# Garden Design

# Alan Titchmarsh
## how to garden

# Garden Design

## BBC
### BOOKS

Published in 2009 by BBC Books, an imprint of
Ebury Publishing, a Random House Group Company

The Random House Group Limited Reg. No. 954009

Addresses for companies within the Random House
Group can be found at
**www.randomhouse.co.uk**

MIX
Paper from responsible sources
FSC® C018179
www.fsc.org

Penguin Random House is committed to a sustainable future
for our business, our readers and our planet. This book is
made from Forest Stewardship Council® certified paper.

A CIP catalogue record for this book is available from
the British Library.

ISBN 978 1 84 6073977

Produced by Outhouse!
Shalbourne, Marlborough, Wiltshire SN8 3QJ

BBC BOOKS
COMMISSIONING EDITORS: Lorna Russell, Stuart Cooper
PROJECT EDITOR: Caroline McArthur
PRODUCTION CONTROLLER: Lucy Harrison

OUTHOUSE!
CONCEPT DEVELOPMENT & PROJECT MANAGEMENT:
  Elizabeth Mallard-Shaw, Sue Gordon
CONTRIBUTING EDITOR: Julia Brittain
PROJECT EDITORS: Lindsey Brown, Anna Kruger
ART DIRECTION: Sharon Cluett, Robin Whitecross
SERIES DESIGN: Sharon Cluett
DESIGNER: Louise Turpin
ILLUSTRATOR: Lizzie Harper

PHOTOGRAPHS by Jonathan Buckley except where
credited otherwise on page 144

Colour origination by Pixel Envy, Italy
Printed and bound in China by Leo Paper Products Ltd.

# Contents

# Introduction

Gardening is one of the best and most fulfilling activities on earth, but it can sometimes seem complicated and confusing. The answers to problems can usually be found in books, but big fat gardening books can be rather daunting. Where do you start? How can you find just the information you want without wading through lots of stuff that is not appropriate to your particular problem? Well, a good index is helpful, but sometimes a smaller book devoted to one particular subject fits the bill better – especially if it is reasonably priced and if you have a small garden where you might not be able to fit in everything suggested in a larger volume.

The *How to Garden* books aim to fill that gap – even if sometimes it may be only a small one. They are clearly set out and written, I hope, in a straightforward, easy-to-understand style. I don't see any point in making gardening complicated, when much of it is based on common sense and observation. (All the key techniques are explained and illustrated, and I've included plenty of tips and tricks of the trade.)

There are suggestions on the best plants and the best varieties to grow in particular situations and for a particular effect. I've tried to keep the information crisp and to the point so that you can find what you need quickly and easily and then put your new-found knowledge into practice. Don't worry if you're not familiar with the Latin names of plants. They are there to make sure you can find the plant as it will be labelled in the nursery or garden centre, but where appropriate I have included common names, too. Forgetting a plant's name need not stand in your way when it comes to being able to grow it.

Above all, the *How to Garden* books are designed to fill you with passion and enthusiasm for your garden and all that its creation and care entails, from designing and planting it to maintaining it and enjoying it. For more than fifty years gardening has been my passion, and that initial enthusiasm for watching plants grow, for trying something new and for just being outside pottering has never faded. If anything I am keener on gardening now than I ever was and get more satisfaction from my plants every day. It's not that I am simply a romantic, but rather that I have learned to look for the good in gardens and in plants, and there is lots to be found. Oh, there are times when I fail – when my plants don't grow as well as they should and I need to try harder. But where would I rather be on a sunny day? Nowhere!

The *How to Garden* handbooks will, I hope, allow some of that enthusiasm – childish though it may be – to rub off on you, and the information they contain will, I hope, make you a better gardener, as well as opening your eyes to the magic of plants and flowers.

# Introducing garden design

Do you ever look at a garden and wonder what it is that makes it successful? It's easy to think it just evolved, as if by magic – the owner has 'green fingers', the site is idyllic, the birds sing there … That may be partly true, but for a garden to work as a whole, there has to be more to it. Every site has its limitations – awkward shape, poor soil, shady aspect – but a good garden will have disguised or overcome these. The plants will be well suited to the situation and someone will have thought about how they would change with time, and how to get the best from them. In short, the garden will have been *designed*. If it doesn't appear that way, then it's a real success.

# Why design matters

Garden design has long been considered a luxury. The grand gardens of the past had designers: if you asked a dozen people to name one famous garden designer, the name Capability Brown would be sure to come up. He has a lot to answer for. Garden design was for the wealthy, with rolling acres to transform, not for the ordinary gardener.

We've come a long way since then, but even now there's a feeling that garden design is some kind of extravagance, an optional extra. Most people have relatively small gardens, and plots are getting smaller. So why, and how, is design relevant or necessary?

Design is about making the best use of the space you have; it's about practicalities and problem-solving. Of course, it's also about producing something that looks pleasing, but, like a building, a successful garden must suit its site and work well for the people who use it. Even the most basic garden will benefit from these design considerations – particularly smaller gardens, where every inch counts. Then there's the question of the garden feeling comfortable and right for *you*.

When you're planning your new garden, you may find it helps to keep a sketchbook for jotting down ideas and plans. Include photos, magazine cuttings – anything that inspires you. It can be very therapeutic!

## Creating a place

Designing a garden involves creating a place. It should be an agreeable place to be, and an interesting space to explore. This will mean different things to different people, but whatever your preferences and tastes, the first step in making a satisfying garden is to create good lines and proportions when you plan it. Understanding how to use shapes, lines and proportions effectively is a fundamental design skill. Another important piece of equipment in the designer's toolbox is an awareness of colour, light and shade – how they work, and how to manipulate them to get the effects you want. A knowledge of plants, their preferences, their behaviour and how to combine them to best effect, is hugely valuable when it comes to finding the right ones for your particular site and situation. So, whether your garden is dry, shady, damp, windy or just plain difficult, don't try to fight it. Keep it simple, work with nature, trust your instincts and begin to transform your space.

Never forget that many an excellent garden began with a difficult site. You'll be amazed how a plot can be transformed by re-thinking the space and choosing appropriate plants.

# Design principles

The last thing anyone wants when they're full of enthusiasm for making a new garden is to be bombarded with a lot of rules. But garden design is about planning spaces, and it has long been accepted that certain basic principles apply to the spaces we find workable, satisfying and 'right'. If you can keep these ideas in your mind (and to many people with design flair they will be second nature), then you're more likely to end up with a garden you like and enjoy living with.

An open, sunnier area beyond a patch of cool, green shade provides contrast and an invitation to move on and explore. Bold foliage shapes and pools of bright colour give balance and seasonal interest.

These tried and tested principles of design relate to proportion, scale, movement and flow, unity, rhythm and balance. They aren't clear-cut, and often overlap. Perhaps the best way to use them is as a check-list when you are evaluating layout possibilities in the early stages. Obviously, they will have to work alongside many other considerations such as practical constraints and your personal tastes, preferences and budget.

## Proportion
Echoing the proportions of your house in the garden's layout often works very well, giving house and garden a sense of belonging to each other. For example, you might use the width of a gable or the footprint of a hexagonal conservatory as a guide to the size and shape of an adjacent terrace or lawn.

Think, too, about the proportions of the different areas and the various features in your garden in relation to each other. A simplified version of the well-known 'golden ratio' – a mathematical and artistic theory used since classical times – can be a useful rule of thumb. Two lines in a certain proportion to each other – roughly speaking, one-third to two-thirds – will tend to give a pleasing effect. Try this 'rule of thirds' when deciding how to divide a space or position an entrance, and keep it in mind when planning the ratio of planting to open space – 1:2, or half as much planted area as open space, will often work out well.

You may be stuck with a plot whose proportions instinctively feel all wrong, but there's no need to despair – there are all sorts of design tricks you can use to help correct this (*see* pages 24–9).

## Scale
People are probably the most important element in the scale equation: a garden feels better as a space if it is on a human scale. Big, open exterior spaces don't feel comfortable or secure to sit in, so smaller areas must be defined within them. Paths and steps need to be a good width – more roomy than their indoor equivalents. Pergolas and arches must be high and spacious enough not to feel oppressive.

Choose plants that are in scale with the spaces they are growing in. A tree at the top of a slope will tend to dwarf everything. Tall perennials won't work in a narrow border, nor tiny plants at the foot of a high wall.

## Movement and flow

This is all about giving an incentive to explore. Particular paving patterns, such as brick paving laid lengthways along a path, seem to propel you along to the next part of the garden. Carefully chosen focal points invite you to walk a bit further. A pool of sunlight beyond a patch of shade is always enticing, while a path disappearing round a bend makes you want to know what lies beyond. A shady pergola can create a sense of mystery, arousing curiosity. Avoid 'dead ends', which discourage any sense of movement.

## Unity

A sense of unity helps prevent your garden from being a haphazard jumble of the things you happen to want or need in it. Elements that give unity to a design include a theme or a style: if the house is contemporary, with clean lines and strong shapes, then carrying this style consistently through into the garden will make it all hang together. As a rule of thumb, formal areas tend to work best nearer the house, informal areas farther away from it. Restraint in your use of materials, shapes and colours can also help to unify a space. Using too many different materials, or a random mix of colours, will have the opposite effect.

## Rhythm

Rhythm in garden design, just as in music, usually entails repetition of a pattern or motif. Repeating a particular plant grouping, or having two or more similar arches, steps, planted pots or other such features

Movement and flow have clearly been thought about in this garden. A series of eye-catching specimen plants and a sculpture provide focal points to lead the eye through the garden, and there is a choice of walking routes to give variety.

at intervals along a path, gives coherence and leads the eye on through the garden.

## Balance

Try to avoid a lopsided effect – the feeling that one side of the garden is dominant as you walk through it.

Tall plants, major groups of plants, and focal points should be evenly distributed to right and left so that both sides look equally important. When planning your planting, take care not to have all the evergreens on one side, or the garden will look unbalanced in winter.

# The site – what have you got?

A garden is rarely an entirely blank canvas. There are usually existing features, and attributes such as climate, aspect, topography and soil need to be considered at the planning stage. However beautiful your design may be in your mind's eye, the reality will be a disappointment if you ignore these 'givens'. Remember – creating a successful garden is as much about problem solving as it is about artistic vision.

Don't underestimate the advantages of a compact, partly shaded urban plot. Shelter can be a real bonus in this kind of garden, creating an ideal microclimate for exotic plants and a jungle effect.

A professional garden designer would carry out a thorough site analysis to investigate and record all the factors above. You may not want to consult a professional, but you should take the time to stand and stare, so you are fully aware of what your garden does. Do overhanging trees cut out light and rainfall? Does the soil become bone dry the moment the sun warms it up in spring? Are there any persistent damp spots? Where are the sunny places, at different times of day – in winter as well as in summer? The answers to questions like these are often your most useful guide in planning a workable layout. They are also invaluable in helping you achieve one of the most important goals in gardening: choosing the right plants for the right places.

## Plot size

The design of your garden will be dictated by the size of the plot, so make a record of its dimensions at an early stage. An empty plot always appears bigger than it really is, and it's easy to think you can fit in more than it will easily accommodate, resulting in a garden that seems overcrowded. With a few rough measurements in front of you it's much easier to be realistic from the outset about what you can include.

## Setting

The best gardens are those that sit well in their surroundings. This applies not only to big plots in the country, with a backdrop of woodland or rolling hills, but also to smaller, urban gardens, which might take their cue from the Victorian terraced house or contemporary studio to which they belong. Make notes and take photographs of the views from your garden – the aspects that will need screening, as well as those that could be adopted into your scheme. Also note the style of adjacent buildings, their materials, and details, which could perhaps be echoed in your design.

## Shape

The shape of a plot can be deceptive. Unless your garden is a simple rectangle it may be worth doing a bit of basic surveying (see pages 18–19) to get a reasonably accurate idea on paper of the shape you are dealing with. In the case of bigger plots, large-scale Ordnance Survey maps may help. These are available online, for a fee, or you can consult them in some public libraries (scales 1:1250 or 1:2500 are the best). Remember, though, that these larger-scale maps are not always up to date, so boundaries may have changed. Aerial photographs can be useful, too. Again, your local library or public record office may be able to help. Some parts of the country are also covered by large-scale satellite photography, accessible online via Google Earth.

As well as recording the actual shape of the plot, note down and perhaps photograph any areas that feel awkward, cramped, inaccessible or generally difficult. They will need special treatment in your planning.

## Topography

A flat, level site is a mixed blessing – it is easier to survey, but harder to make into an interesting three-dimensional garden. A sloping site entails more work if you need to make terraces or steps (*see* pages 16–17), but it can lend character to a garden, offering effortless changes of eye-level as well as contrasting views of the immediate landscape when going along the same path in different directions.

## Aspect and orientation

These will be key factors in your design. Use a compass to find north, and record where the sun falls at different times of day, ideally in both summer and in winter. This will help you plan seating areas, and it will be a valuable guide for siting new trees and other tall features where they won't cast unwanted shade. Equally important, knowing which areas are sunny or shady is essential when it comes to choosing plants. Note the different types of shade, such as gloomy areas beneath deciduous trees where there will be more light in winter when the trees are bare, but where the soil is also likely to be dry and poor. On the north side of a building, or beneath evergreens, there may well be year-round shade. Earmark any protected, 'sun-trap' areas as possible locations for plants (and people!) that love to bask.

Dappled shade around deciduous trees (here a tulip tree, *Liriodendron tulipifera*) can be a lovely effect to create. The space will be sunny in winter and inviting in a different way in summer, when the leafy canopy tempers the sun's heat and glare.

Wind direction will also be a factor, determining whether you will need to create shelter in certain areas (*see also* pages 132–3).

## Climate and microclimate

Different gardens – or even parts of the same garden – have their own climatic conditions, a fact that is largely the result of aspect and orientation. Other factors, such as the surrounding topography, play their part too. For example, 'frost pockets' are particular areas that seem especially prone to frost, possibly due to some obstruction that prevents cold air from draining away down a slope. It may not be possible to 'cure' a frost pocket, but if you have identified it at least you'll know not to put vulnerable plants there. The same applies to damp spots, or places where buildings cause wind turbulence. The most successful planning and planting will take factors like these into account at an early stage.

## Drainage

You'll probably be only too familiar with how your garden behaves in very wet weather. If drainage is poor, note where the worst places are, and consider installing land drains if the problem is really severe (*see* pages 136–7). Terracing slopes to make level, absorbent surfaces will help solve any problems there may be with excessive water run-off (*see* pages 16–17).

## Soil

The type of soil you have is critical in choosing the right plants. The most important thing to find out is whether your soil drains freely (more likely on sand or chalk) or retains moisture (probably on clay). Whether the soil is acid or alkaline makes a big difference to certain plants. Many rhododendrons and camellias, and some heathers, magnolias and other popular shrubs and trees, dislike alkaline soil. Other plants – clematis, pinks and many shrubby herbs – just love it. Improving the soil in a general way is always worthwhile, but with extreme soil types it is usually best to choose plants that suit the soil you have, rather than trying to change the character of your soil radically to suit the plants.

Observation is a good rough guide to basic soil type. Notice how the soil behaves, whether existing plants (including weeds) grow well in it, and what it looks and feels like in different weather conditions. Can you dig after heavy rain without soil sticking to everything? Do puddles hang around for days? Do you tend to lose plants through summer drought or winter waterlogging? Which plants appear to grow well in neighbouring gardens?

Greater precision than this may not be necessary, and more scientific soil testing is often less helpful than you might think because soil can vary quite a lot in different parts of a garden. For example, chalky soils sometimes have a 'clay cap' which makes the ground heavy and sticky in places, while acid soil can become more alkaline near buildings and paving, where there may be old mortar rubble. However, if you want to know the precise pH of your soil, testing kits are widely available.

Shingle and dense, drought-tolerant planting – a classic, practical solution that has made a success of many a sun-baked garden with poor, dry soil.

## Existing plants

When taking over an existing garden, it is certainly worth saving any decent plants, especially mature trees and shrubs, that are already growing and can be renovated. Even if they would not be your first choice, they will prevent a feeling of bareness in the new garden and give it a sense of maturity from the outset. Make a list of the trees and shrubs you think may be worth preserving. This will also help you to reduce your plant bill.

## Existing buildings and hard landscaping

Think about what you could do with existing garden buildings, fencing and other hard landscape structures: could they be restored, or just given a coat of paint, to make them useful in a new scheme? You may be able to save on costs by reusing existing paving, either in situ – perhaps with a new edging, different detailing or a change of emphasis – or elsewhere in the garden. Recycled paving slabs or shingle can be useful for making hard paths in a kitchen garden, or around a greenhouse, shed or compost area. Consider all the possibilities before you decide to scrap any of the structures or materials you have on the site.

Make a note of any eyesores that need to be disguised or concealed, such as an oil tank or a neighbour's shed. There are ways to screen them. (*See* pages 100–1 for ideas.)

## Underground services

It is vital to establish the location and depth of any pipework or cabling that crosses the site so that you can work round it, if possible. Relocating services can be a costly operation, and with careful planning you can usually avoid it. Recently installed electricity cables, water mains and other services should have been laid to a statutory safe depth and be suitably protected, so they may not cause problems, but it's a good idea to find out where you may need to take special care when digging – inadvertent damage could have expensive consequences. With newer properties, you may be

able to get hold of the architect's plan of the site showing the routes of services. Otherwise, the location of inspection covers and visible pipes and cables may offer clues.

**Don't forget**

You will probably have to work round existing access points to and from the house and the road, so doors and gates must be factored into your layout at an early stage. People tend to take the shortest route from A to B, even if it means cutting corners, so position paths on, or very close to, these routes.

Beth Chatto's wonderful garden sits on an unpromising combination of wet clay and dry gravel. Her secret? Choose plants to suit the conditions.

On a sloping site you'll need at least some areas of level ground. Creating these is likely to involve an expensive upheaval, but take heart. Imaginatively planned changes of level will not only make your garden more practical, but will give you a much more interesting space. You can turn the slope to advantage and use terraces, banks and steps to divide the space in ways that will be useful, pleasing to look at and tailor-made to your own needs.

### Terracing

This involves moving earth to create level areas, each contained on the downhill side by a retaining wall or bank. It is a major undertaking, and for anything more ambitious than simple terracing of a shallow slope you should definitely get professional advice from a landscape architect or a building contractor. A retaining wall, especially if it is more than 1m (40in) high, has to bear a considerable load and must be properly reinforced. It's important to get the drainage right, too, or water may build up behind the wall in wet weather, putting more pressure on the structure and even risking collapse.

Nevertheless, terracing can be a really worthwhile solution that makes the most of limited space and helps connect a house with its garden. Often a low retaining wall is all that's needed. It doesn't have to be straight: a curve may suit the site, and you can soften the line with planting or break it up with steps, seating or a water feature. If your house is at the top of the slope, terraces will present the garden to the house, but should your house be at the bottom, you may be better off working with the slope, rather than looking at a series of brick 'risers' like a flight of steps.

### Banks

A bank is easier to construct than a retaining wall, but takes up more space. It's advisable to make the bank no steeper than 1 in 2 (30 degrees), so for a bank 1m high you need a 2m horizontal space. Banks steeper than this will be difficult to maintain or mow, and the steeper the bank the more likely it is that soil will creep gradually downhill.

Banks can be either grassed over or planted. If you decide on grass, include some dwarf bulbs – a flowery bank is a cheering sight in spring. If you would prefer a covering of plants, make sure

Contemporary terracing for a sunny, dry slope: timber sleepers and a mulch of cobbles. In a terraced garden, year-round planting softens the impact of retaining walls, which can hit the eye when viewed from the bottom of a steep slope.

## Planting to overhang walls

Plants that loll comfortably over the top of a wall from the bed above give a relaxed effect and help soften the hard line of the wall. Where possible, leave plenty of space for plants to overhang without getting in the way. Fragrant plants work well, being within easy reach for brushing against and sniffing. A bed at the top of a sunny wall is likely to be very well drained, so this would be an excellent place for drought-tolerant Mediterranean herbs such as hyssop, prostrate rosemary, lavender and thyme. Other plants to try include *Centranthus ruber*, *Convolvulus cneorum* and *Erigeron karvinskianus* (all below) and low, spreading cultivars of cistus, anthemis and artemisia.

some of your choices are perennials with fibrous, mat-forming root systems, such as *Alchemilla mollis, Geranium macrorrhizum, Heuchera* or *Tellima grandiflora*, to help hold the soil in place. You can also plant some low, spreading shrubs, perhaps *Cotoneaster dammeri* or *Lonicera pileata*, or creepers such as periwinkles and variegated ivies. Ground-cover planting keeps maintenance low, and rain won't wash loose earth down the slope when you disturb the soil by clearing or weeding.

## Steps

Steps are often needed to link different levels, and there are so many attractive ways to build them it's a pity not to make them a focal feature. Spend a bit of time considering the options, both formal and informal, and the choice of materials. And don't forget safety considerations too. (*See also* page 47.)

## Ramps

A ramp has to slope more gently than steps so it takes up more space, but it may be a better option in terms of

access with a mower or wheelbarrow, or for anyone with limited mobility. The width of the ramp will depend on its intended use. The ramp could be L-shaped, or it could consist of two parallel runs with a 'landing' half-way, like a hairpin bend. It may be built alongside steps. Remember to use a textured surface, as a smooth one can be slippery when wet. Try a bonded aggregate, rough-textured bricks or setts, or ridged paving slabs.

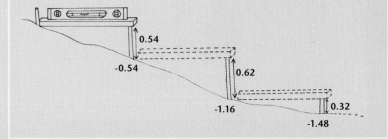

Changes of level around natural ponds need a light touch. ① Grass studded with primroses and wood anemones is just right for Great Dixter's Lower Moat. ② A froth of informal planting softens the steps in a more contemporary garden.

**Taking levels**

When you're planning steps and terraces you will need at least a rough idea of the level changes. There are numerous pieces of kit for measuring levels, from an old-fashioned spirit level to state-of-the-art laser technology. The fall of a slope can be plotted approximately by measuring the fall in an adjacent fence or wall, or (as below) by recording the drop at 1m (40in) intervals using a plank, a spirit level and a vertical rule.

0.54

-0.54

0.62

-1.16

0.32

-1.48

# Your garden on paper

Making a plan can be a useful way to begin creating a garden design, but it isn't essential. Some lucky people are blessed with the ability to walk round a garden, immediately see what's wrong and visualize a cracking new layout. (This, incidentally, is usually much easier to do in other people's gardens than in your own!) Others feel daunted by the very idea of measuring, plotting and drawing, and would avoid planning their garden at all if that's what they had to do.

Nevertheless, a design plan – even a rough one – drawn to scale on paper can be a tremendously helpful tool. It gives you an idea of whether everything fits (before you start building or planting, and find that it doesn't), and you can play around with shapes and sizes in a way that's difficult to do on the ground. It's also a good basis for calculating fairly accurately the quantities of materials to order for hard landscaping, and it gives you a ready-made template for drawing up a planting plan and estimating the number of plants you will need.

In your survey, you'll need to plot the positions of all the existing features that will affect your design: paths, drives, fences, mature trees and inspection covers.

## Measuring a plot

If you do decide to make a design plan of the whole garden, you will need a clear idea of the shape of the plot, its boundaries and the position of any important features: the house, outbuildings, trees, access points and so on. Surveying can be a complicated business, with different methods and increasingly sophisticated technology. The subject could easily fill a book on its own, so it is not covered in detail here. However, if your garden has a reasonably straightforward shape, you can use some simple surveying techniques to plot its outline on paper. For larger or more complicated gardens, or if you feel you would like to plan the garden on paper but aren't confident about measuring up, consider having a professional survey done. (*See also* pages 12–13 for other possible sources of information on your plot.)

The simplest, most accurate low-tech method of plotting a garden's boundaries and features is to use the classic surveying technique of triangulation, where you plot a point by measuring its distance from two different, known points on a base line. You can use the house wall as your base line, and the two corners

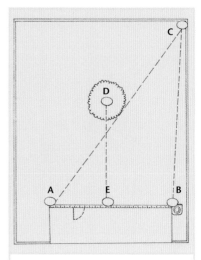

The diagram shows how to plot the corner of the site (C) by triangulation from points A and B, while the tree (D) is plotted as an offset from point (E) on the base line (AB).

## Don't forget

Use metric measurements when drawing up your plan, or you will need to convert everything before you order the materials. These days, off-the-peg items, such as paving slabs, are nearly always supplied in metric sizes, with no imperial equivalents.

of the house as the points from which you measure (*see* the diagram above). First, stretch a tape measure along the wall from one end (A) to the other (B) and note down the distances from A of all doors and windows, and of the house corner (B). Then list the features you intend to plot, for example the corners of the garden (such as C), any other points where the boundaries change direction, and any significant features you plan to keep – such as a shed or greenhouse, a pond or tree. Next, fix the end of the tape at point A and measure the distance to each

Use a retractable metal tape measure for distances up to 5m (16ft) or so. For a whole garden, a surveyor's tape (up to 50m/165ft long) is best.

### MAKE A WISH LIST

In creating the new garden of your dreams, it's surprisingly easy to lose sight of some of the practical things you want to achieve. So, at the outset, make a wish list of the features that you would like to have in your new garden. For a family garden, for example, your list might look like the one below – and your sketch plan could end up looking something like the one on the right.

1  A family dining area, with overhead shade, for outdoor lunches in summer
2  A water feature that can be seen from the kitchen window
3  A wildlife corner, where visiting birds can be seen from the house in winter
4  Overhead screening (a pergola) from a neighbour's upstairs window
5  Secure but attractive boundaries to keep children and dogs safe
6  A level, well-drained, grassy play area with sun for most of the year
7  A seat in the sun for morning coffee, or for a summer evening drink
8  An unobtrusive (but not too shady) place to dry the washing
9  An easy-maintenance raised bed for herbs and salad crops
10  Accessible but tucked-away storage for bicycles and tools

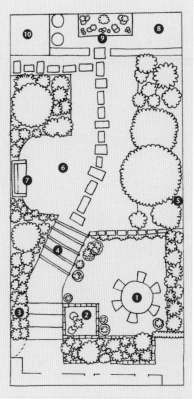

of the features on your list. Then fix the end of the tape at point B and record the distance from there to each feature. Finally, measure the footprint of any structures, and note down the diameter of the canopy of trees and major shrubs.

For plotting other features in the garden, a quicker but less accurate method is to take 'offsets' from the base line. Measure and record the distance from each feature (such as the tree, D) to the base line, being careful to make sure the tape meets the base line at right angles. Record the distance from the start of the base line (A) to the point where the offset tape meets it (E).

You can then replicate your measurements on paper, using a scale rule and a set square as described below.

## Plotting the site

Armed with your measurements, and back at your work table, the next step is to turn the information you have collected into a rough site plan. You'll need a sharp pencil, a large sheet of paper, a scale rule, a set square and a pair of compasses (oh, and an eraser!). First, decide on a scale. Use the largest scale you can without making the plan unwieldy. For a small garden a scale of 1:50 will do very nicely (that is, 1cm on the plan = 50cm on the site).

Using your scale rule, draw in your base line to the correct length. Then, again using your scale rule, set the compasses to the distance from

A to your first feature. Draw an arc representing that distance from A. Do the same with the distance from B to the feature. Where the arcs cross is the position of the feature.

Build up a master plan of the garden's shape and features in this way, then make some photocopies to use as templates on to which you can roughly sketch all your design ideas.

You are now all set to experiment with as many different layouts as it takes to find the one that ticks all the boxes. *See* pages 24–9 for some design tips that may help you to get started on a layout. You will get there in the end.

## Planting plans

When you've decided on a layout for the plot – whether or not you've made a design plan – it's definitely worth taking the trouble to make a planting plan for each bed and border in your garden.

On paper – away from the lures of the garden centre – it's much easier to assess how much space each plant will take up, what you can plant underneath what, how many plants of each kind you'll need, and what the effect will be throughout the year. Think about the long-term suitability of each plant, and the best combinations and groupings. The result will be more satisfying this way, and the saving you'll make on all the unsuitable impulse buys you've avoided will pay for a few more plants that will be just right.

## Measuring beds and borders

A planting plan needn't be fancy, but it does need to be roughly to scale (1:50 is usually best), so measure and draw an accurate outline of each bed. Measuring a single flower bed is a piece of cake in comparison with surveying a whole garden. Rectangular beds are the easiest, of course, but do measure all four sides, as what looks like a rectangle won't always be true. For borders with one irregular side, run a tape along the straight side and then measure out from this at right angles, at 1m intervals, plotting corresponding points along the edge on the other side.

Having measured the shape of the bed, plot the dimensions on paper. Use a circle template to draw in the

plants; at 1:50 a shrub with a diameter of 1m will be represented as a circle 20mm across. Size is a knotty problem here: do you draw a tree or shrub at the size it is when you plant it, or at its eventual size? The best answer is a compromise. So a medium-sized shrub that might reach a diameter of 1.5m (5ft) within two to five years of planting would be shown by a circle 30mm across.

Label each circle as you go with the name of the plant, or number them and use a key. Link the circles representing plants of the same kind that form a group, so you only have to write the name once. You may like to sketch in a bit of detail to remind you at a glance what each plant is: jagged edges for a spiky plant like a yucca, tiny dots for a clipped box, billowy outlines for a rose. Position trees and evergreen shrubs first. It's important to get these in just the right place because

they will be with you for a long time. Shade in any evergreen shrubs that reach right down to the ground, as they won't need any underplanting. Overlap the circles where one plant is beneath another, for example a shrub beneath a tree and then a herbaceous plant at

**PLANTING PLAN FOR A 6 × 2M (20 × 6FT) SUNNY BORDER**
Evergreen shrubs and grasses give structure and all-year interest. Flowering shrubs and perennials, underplanted with spring bulbs, are chosen for seasonal succession.

1 *Philadelphus* 'Silberregen'
2 *Aquilegia alpina* (×6)
3 *Buxus sempervirens* 'Elegantissima'
4 *Yucca filamentosa* 'Bright Edge' (×3)
5 *Euphorbia characias* subsp. *wulfenii* (×2)
6 *Narcissus* 'Jack Snipe' (×50)

7 *Rosa* 'Winchester Cathedral' (×2)
8 *Helianthemum* 'Wisley White' (×2)
9 *Geranium* 'Rozanne' (×5)
10 *Stipa tenuissima* (×5)
11 *Mahonia × media* 'Winter Sun'
12 *Osmanthus heterophyllus* 'Goshiki'

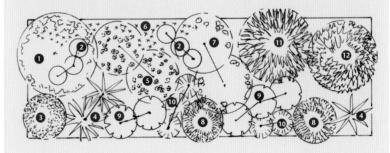

ground level. Bulbs can be shown as drifts of dots or little crosses.

Finally, list all the plants on the plan, with quantities of each. That's your shopping list.

## From paper to garden

To transfer a design or a planting layout from a plan to the ground, start by converting some of the key measurements to real distances on the ground, and write them on the plan. With a planting plan, this might be the distance along the border – and the distance from the back – of the key plants, such as trees and large or evergreen shrubs. Position these key plants, in their pots, in the bed, and use them as a guide for placing the rest of the plants. You needn't measure the exact position for every single one.

Similarly, with a design plan, plot several points along the outline of a proposed path, patio or pond, for example, and join them to mark the outline with pegs and string, or with a hosepipe fixed to the ground with wire pegs or hoops. Use long canes to mark the positions of trees and other tall features, to give you a general idea of how the layout will look. As you mark out more features, it becomes easier to locate the rest. Live with this rough layout for a few days, look at it from every angle, imagine it in every kind of light and weather. When you're finally happy, mark it out more permanently with paint or a trail of dry sand.

A plastic bottle filled with free-running dry sand is a handy way of marking your layout on the ground.

If a planting plan seems a bother, remember that it is usually a much surer route to a well-designed border, with shapes and colours working well together, and the right plants in the right places.

# Your garden from the window

In the course of an average year, even the keenest gardener will probably spend less time working or sitting in the garden than looking at it from indoors. Your garden may well be your first glimpse of the outside world when you wake up in the morning, and your last before closing the curtains at dusk. How the garden is seen from the house is critical, so it's definitely worth a bit of effort to make the picture a pleasing one.

## Planning your views

Making the house an integral part of your garden scheme begins with looking out of the windows and doors, long and hard, at various times of day and in different lights, weathers and seasons. Take photographs and make notes. What would you like to be looking at? Think about which views you want to preserve, and those you would rather not see, so that you can plan appropriate screening. Consider how you could align paths and other features to enhance the views from the house. A long, framed vista could perhaps give the illusion of more space,

Never, ever forget the view from indoors! ① Planting in front of a window looks attractive and luxuriant, but be ready to trim plants if they keep out the light. ② Think about which windows you look out of most, and create pleasing views to enjoy all year round.

while a path disappearing round
a corner lends a sense of mystery.

## Come into the garden

There's nothing better on a warm
summer's morning than to have the
door open and the garden beckoning.
An inviting focal point visible from the
doorway works well as an enticement
to step outside, as do special, one-off
plants that demand closer inspection.
Blurring the boundary between inside
and out has the same effect; you
could do this by growing climbers
and creepers around windows and
doorways, or paving the area outside
the door with a material similar to the
flooring inside. Planted containers
grouped close to the door give a sense
of abundance and enable you to ring
the changes with the seasons: spring
bulbs are a particular pleasure grown
in this way, and will be protected from
the worst effects of the elements.

## Bringing the view to life

In late winter, plants that change
ever so slightly each day, heralding
spring, are a treat to watch from the
windows – emerging snowdrops, of
course, and winter aconites and early
scillas. Euphorbias such as *Euphorbia
characias* subsp. *wulfenii* slowly unfurl
acid-green flowerheads very early in
the year. The winter-flowering tree
*Prunus* x *subhirtella* 'Autumnalis' is
compact enough to grow quite near
the house, and will keep your spirits
up all winter with its flushes of delicate
white blossom whenever the weather
turns mild. Certain grasses, such as
miscanthus or *Stipa tenuissima*, and
other plants that move easily with the
wind such as catkin-bearing shrubs and
trees, bring movement and incident to

Provide the birds with plenty of cover,
fresh water and a varied food supply of
nuts, seeds and berries. In return their
visits will enliven your garden on every
day of the year.

the scene – all helping to keep the
interest going in different ways.

Watching birds from the house is
such a privilege that it is worth making
special arrangements for them – not
only conveniently positioned feeders,
nestboxes, and water for drinking and
bathing, but also plants that they will
appreciate, visible from your windows.
Small birds such as blue tits and wrens
like to patrol shrubs for tiny insects,
while blackbirds are attracted by the
winter berries of pyracantha and
cotoneaster. Don't forget upstairs.
One summer evening you may be
lucky enough to see an elephant
hawkmoth, all glamorous and pink,
feeding on the nectar of a honeysuckle
outside your bedroom window.

Garden fragrance is famously elusive,
often catching you unawares. Position
fragrant plants carefully to get maximum
benefit from these pleasant surprises,
planting near windows and doors so
that the perfume can waft indoors. The
swooning scent of a daphne on a sunny
spring afternoon, or of jasmine on a
balmy evening, can make your day, and
just a little planning will see it happen.
It's lovely to let summer night-time
fragrance drift in through open
windows. Honeysuckle (below bottom),
jasmine or *Trachelospermum jasminoides*
over a porch or pergola will do the trick.
Beds and containers can be filled with
*Lilium regale* or scented annuals such as
heliotrope, with its rich cherry aroma,
*Nicotiana* (tobacco plant), or night-
scented stocks for a tight space.
A raised bed of aromatic Mediterranean
herbs such as lavender, thyme and
rosemary will thrive in a warm sunny
corner, no matter how poor the soil.

Several fragrant winter- and spring-
flowering shrubs are compact enough
to grow around doors and windows. Try
the white-flowered *Sarcococca confusa*
(below top) beneath a window on a
north-facing wall, or a daphne where
there is a bit more sun. The larger
deciduous shrubs *Abeliophyllum distichum*
and *Chimonanthus praecox* are just as free
with their winter and early spring
perfume. Plant them where there is an
empty stretch of sunny wall to train
them on, and partner them with
a summer-flowering clematis to scramble
through their branches. For shadier
spots, plant a mint or lily-of-the-valley.

# Garden shapes

Beautiful gardens can be made on plots of any shape and size. Of course, there is no substitute for a well-proportioned space – but most gardens don't start out that way. Whether yours is standard-issue rectangular or the wackiest mix of angles or curves, you can use all sorts of tricks to alter, or enhance, its apparent size and shape. Most shapes have their pros and cons – to achieve a good layout, you just have to make sure the pros win the day.

Amazingly, this garden is only 14m (45ft) square. Strong shapes, good verticals and action-packed planting distract you from the boundaries. There's more interest here than in most gardens several times as big.

## Thinking outside the box

Whatever you do, don't make the perimeter the starting point for your new design. Following the boundary lines will emphasize the shape of the plot and make it look smaller. Never, ever make narrow borders along the fences, leaving what's left as a lawn in the middle. Start, instead, from the other end of the telescope. Think not in terms of boundaries but in terms of open spaces – even small ones.

So, plan well-defined, strongly shaped spaces for the heart of your plot. The best take their cue from the shapes and proportions of the house, giving house and garden a clear sense of unity, which can be reinforced through your choice of hard landscaping materials (*see* pages 52–5). Other strong shapes might include a lawn in the shape of a circle, or two circles or diagonally positioned rectangles that interlock with each other.

Having determined the open areas, start to plan planting and features to give your layout structure and purpose, and to fill any 'dead space' left around the edges. This will distract attention from the garden's shape and blur the boundaries.

## Using space creatively

On all but the tiniest plot, plan a walkable route so that you can stroll into the garden and return to the house a different way. It needn't all be a major path. Part of the route could cross an open space such as a lawn or paved area, and stepping-stones or narrow, bark-surfaced paths could form part of the circuit. Plan a series of interesting things along the way – specimen plants, seats, containers, a water feature – each one leading to the next.

Use changes of level to define separate areas. These can either be created by terracing an existing slope (*see* pages 16–17), or contrived artificially on a flat site (but don't forget that for every up there will have to be a corresponding down).

Contrasting areas of light and shade can bring changes of mood and invite you to walk on. Light and shade, and colour, can also be used to alter the apparent shape of a space by creating the illusion of distance and depth (*see also* page 83). Dark colours tend to recede while light colours appear nearer. You'll be amazed at the effect of painting structures black, for example; it makes a fence or shed virtually disappear. Black also makes a flattering backdrop to planting in front of it – useful for creating a sense of depth. Golden or silver foliage, or architectural plants, look really striking with a black backdrop, as do shapely bare twigs or frost-covered seedheads, enhanced by low winter sunshine.

Keeping just one long view will give an impression of distance and space in the garden. It doesn't have to be a main path: any clear sight line will do, perhaps with a focal point just visible at the far end.

Mirrors are useful tools for giving the impression of a larger space, but must be at just the right angle, and set among planting or behind trellis, to hide the edges and make the illusion work.

## The awkward shape

For all sorts of reasons, some gardens are just a funny shape. Boundaries may have changed over the years, and bits of land been acquired or sold off, or sheds demolished, or a house extended. The shape of a house and its position on a plot can leave you with an awkward space, or even a whole series of them, but applying some of the techniques outlined above can help turn the situation to advantage. An awkward plot outline can prompt inventive ways of creating spaces within it that will make a more interesting and original garden than a 'standard' site such as a square or oblong. You'll soon forget you ever thought you had a difficult site.

### Tips and tricks

- If you can't see the whole of a space at once, it will feel larger.
- Looking down a slope or a step makes a given area seem longer.
- An open area feels sunnier if you go through shade to reach it.
- A narrow entrance into a space will make the space feel bigger when you get there.
- A path that narrows slightly as you walk (or look) along it feels longer.
- The direction in which paving bricks or slabs are laid can make a path look longer (if they are laid lengthways) or wider (if laid crosswise).
- Still water, with its reflective surface, makes a space appear larger.

A stone lion framed by formal hedging is a focal point across the lawn, with an 'avenue' of topiary to lead the eye. The long view gives the impression of a larger space.

## Square gardens

A square garden may be dead easy to measure and to plot on paper especially if it's flat, but it can be quite a challenge to turn it into something interesting. Clever planting will be one of your best allies, along with thinking in three dimensions and using strong shapes like diagonals or curves. Experiment with hexagons or octagons too – they will connect with the formal lines of the square while introducing a different directional pull.

### Divide and conquer

Breaking up the garden into distinct areas is the first step in overcoming the predictability of a square space, but this needs to be done very subtly so the divisions don't look too contrived. Planting is often the best way – it's amazingly versatile and a welcome natural touch to complement and contrast with the geometry. Use plants, such as a

tree or bamboo, to create height; separate spaces at a low level with a dwarf box hedge (or *Euonymus japonicus* 'Microphyllus' if box blight is a problem); or use tall grasses, the slender-stemmed *Verbena bonariensis* or a climber on a trellis to act as a semi-transparent screen.

Screens used to divide a garden don't need to be solid. Trellis is often ideal, allowing light and air to pass through and giving climbing plants an instant foothold.

### Courtyard gardens

Though often square, these are less problematic than larger square gardens because there won't be room for major divisions of the space, and the scale is intimate enough for a real 'outdoor room'. Contemporary design (*see* pages 32–3) works very well for a courtyard garden. You'll find inspiration in the great variety of small gardens built each year for the Chelsea Flower Show. The most successful ones are those that bring together several features or incidents – perhaps a welcoming entrance, a seating area, a water feature and some cracking planting – into a coherent whole, with a unifying design theme that runs through the colours, materials and shapes used. You can create elements of surprise by having small areas hidden by planting, or by tucking a sculpture or unusual specimen plant into a corner where it can only be seen from certain angles.

### Three dimensions

Height and levels are more important than ever in a square garden. If possible, set at least one part of the garden at a different level – perhaps a raised bed or semi-raised pond. Even a single low step makes a big difference if its position and shape emphasize the structure and proportions of your garden.

### Long, narrow gardens

Long and narrow is without doubt the most common 'problem' shape for a garden. Look out of a train window as you go through older areas of towns and cities and you'll see them by the dozen. In the case of terraced houses, the garden will usually be the same width as the dwelling; with semi-detached houses it will be a little wider.

Curves and circles here counteract the 'boxiness' of a square plot. There are raised seating areas (1) and (3), with a screened utility area (4), and a pergola (1) and trees (2) for height.

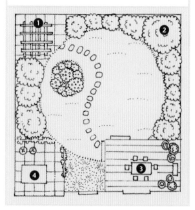

Either way, it's all too easy for the garden to look and feel like a passageway, particularly when there are tall wooden fences on either side and a long straight path to the end.

## Making compartments

What you need to do is to turn the garden – both physically and visually – into a place to linger in, rather than one to rush through.

The tried and tested trick of dividing up the space will work a treat here. Think of the garden as a series of smaller spaces, each one related to and leading on to the next. This feeling of connectedness can be achieved by repeating hard landscape materials, or colours or particular plants. An element of the unexpected will be important as you enter the different areas, so ensure

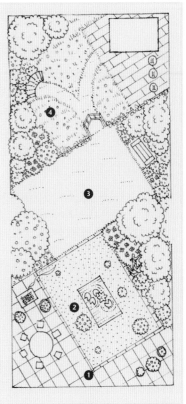

A narrow garden becomes a series of linked areas set diagonally crosswise. A patio (1) overlooks a gravel area with a pond (2), leading to a lawn (3), then through an arch to a meadow area (4).

A winding path through dense, varied planting within a framework of evergreens completely hides the boundaries of this narrow town garden.

that at least part of each space is hidden. Then consider what you want from the garden and what form you would like each area to take. Your chosen combination might be a romantic, fragrant flower garden, a play area and a compact kitchen garden; or a contemporary dining and barbecue area, a lawn with a couple of fruit trees and a small water garden. Compartments need to be linked to form a coherent whole, but preferably not by means of a straight line. Experiment with different ways of interlocking the shapes, and use diagonals, S shapes and other curves as a distraction from the parallel boundaries.

## Pushing the boundaries sideways

Take every opportunity to emphasize the plot's width – perhaps by having a seat and a focal point at opposite ends of a paved or grassed area that runs across the garden, or by using a mirror to create the illusion of a space beyond the boundary. Incorporate sideways or diagonal views of things outside the garden if you can – a neighbour's tree, a distant landscape or just a patch of sky. Use trees or a structure such as an arch or pergola to lead the eye to these 'borrowed' features. And finally, use plants to disguise fences. If at all possible, make a visual link between your planting and trees or shrubs outside your garden – it will give the illusion of a much bigger planted area and help to make your boundary disappear altogether.

## Triangular gardens

OK, so there may not be many gardens in the shape of a perfect triangle. But if you include all the odd-shaped plots with converging boundaries, plus the wedge-shaped pieces of garden that get left when a house is awkwardly angled on its site, they add up to a significant number of design challenges. Just as with other difficult plot shapes, the solution lies in using strong shapes to focus attention completely within the garden rather than on its corners and boundaries.

A reflective pool gives this inspired London garden another dimension. Vertical plants focus attention within the garden, while the neighbours' 'borrowed' trees blur the boundaries.

## Making the most of it

With any irregularly shaped garden, figure out how to make the best use of the longest dimensions, in order to make the plot look larger. One way is to base your layout on an irregular cross shape, with the two axes running at right angles across the widest part and down the longest part of the garden. Use clever planting to create the illusion that the garden is as wide and as long as this all over, rather than

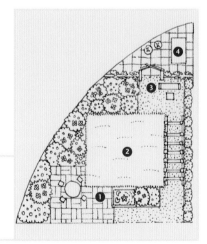

Rectangles for a triangular plot: a patio (1) opens to a lawn (2), which is linked to a gravel area with a pergola (3) – a long axial view. The 'dead end' becomes a screened utility area (4).

disappearing into – literally – the thin end of the wedge. Other shapes to consider are overlapping circles or squares of different sizes, or an elongated octagon or hexagon. Mirrors can also be used to make the narrow end of the plot look wider.

## Wide, shallow gardens

These gardens can make you feel short of 'breathing space', with a neighbour's fence uncomfortably close to your windows. Front gardens, too, are often wide and shallow, but they tend to be less enclosed than back gardens, so the shape is less of a problem.

### Creating depth

The priority with a shallow garden is to create an illusion of depth and distance. Some of the techniques for long, narrow gardens (*see* pages 26–8) work equally well turned through 90 degrees. Borrow views from beyond your garden, and use every trick in the book to make the far boundary recede or disappear. You can manipulate perspective by making a path that leads towards

Creating depth and distance: a clematis-clad arch leads into an open area which narrows into a path disappearing into shade.

the boundary slightly narrower as it runs from the house to the fence – apparently lengthening it. Changes in mood or light along a path – such as the alternating sequence of light and shade that you get beneath a pergola or along an avenue of trees – also appear to increase distance. Planting will be a key part of the illusion; you can choose and position plants to create depth (*see also* page 83) – a light-coloured shrub against a dark yew hedge or conifer will

make the distance between the two plants appear greater than it is.

### The third dimension

Height too can be used as a distraction. Tall, vertical plants and structures to the sides of the garden, contrasted with shorter, horizontal ones along the end boundary, will bring the sides in and appear to lengthen the plot. Tall, interestingly shaped plants grouped around a feature at ground level, such as a pond, will subtly draw attention downwards. Tricks like this help to keep the focus of your vision firmly within the garden rather than on the too-close boundary.

Tall planting (1), (2) and (3) brings in the sides of this wide garden, contrasting with a circle of low planting (4) around a bird bath. The deck timbers (5) are laid lengthways to suggest depth.

Front gardens can be quite a challenge. They are demanding in terms of practicalities – access, parking and so on – but they need to look good because they are constantly on view and they give that important first impression to visitors. They can also give pleasure to passers-by. However, you yourself probably spend little time in your front garden, other than when you're coming in and going out, so it should be relatively undemanding to maintain.

### Parking and practicalities

Parking space will probably have to be accommodated, and perhaps access to a garage (which may not be a pretty sight, especially when its doors are open) and to the back of the house. Other requirements will include clear access to the front door, and perhaps some screening to shield you from road noise and the gaze of people going past your house. Consider all these practicalities first. Be ready to abandon an existing layout if you feel it doesn't work – though if you can make use of existing features, such as a mature hedge or a change of level, it will make the job easier and give your new-look frontage a head start. Try not to let cars dominate the entrance to the house. If there's space to tuck them out of sight, think about making a parking area distinct from the entrance and perhaps shielded, at least partly, by evergreen planting. Make sure you leave sight lines clear for cars to exit safely into the road.

Simple, no-fuss planting is best in a front garden, where you may not want to spend much time on maintenance. ① Euphorbias and phormiums will give strong year-round structure to a sunny front garden. ② Variegated ivy and hostas in containers make a stylish and welcoming entrance around a shady front door.

Imagine how different these two front entrances would look without their plants. ① Harsh concrete steps are much improved by the varied evergreens in containers. ② Exuberant and exotic planting transforms a tucked-away entrance into an inviting oasis.

## Making an entrance

The focal point of a front garden should be the entrance to the house – rather than the garage or parked cars. Suitable planting and lighting will help here. Placing container plants around the front door is a good idea. They make the entrance look welcoming and cared for, and they can be planted with different combinations through the year, so that there is always something looking its best. Keep permanent planting in the front garden simple, with structure – such as evergreen shrubs – where it's needed, and good ground cover. Remember that it will be seen every day of the year, so include plants that have winter interest such as unexpected fragrance or surprisingly colourful flowers even on gloomy days.

## Permeable surfaces

The key issue of the moment for front gardens is the alarming rate at which they are being lost in order to create parking space. UK planning legislation changed in the wake of the floods of 2007, when many properties flooded because run-off from driveways overloaded urban drainage systems. Now, you may find that you are no longer able to cover your front garden with an impermeable surface without planning permission, so tarmac, concrete and mortared paving are out. However, there are several other options if you need a parking space.

### GRAVEL
Cheap and easy to lay, aggregates such as shingle or chippings give a reasonably firm surface that can be driven on and that will absorb rainwater rather than creating run-off problems. There is a wide choice of materials and colours, from pea-shingle to slate or limestone chippings. Gravel is also an effective security measure: it is noisy to walk on and this can deter potential intruders.

### PERMEABLE BLOCK PAVING
Some types of block paving are designed to allow rainwater to escape through the unmortared joints and into the sand layer beneath. You can achieve a similar effect by using various combinations of paving units and aggregates, such as setts or cobbles set into shingle or chippings.

### REINFORCED GRASS
Most useful for areas where cars are not parked permanently, this works by reinforcing the ground with concrete or plastic cellular units or netting, into which soil and grass seed are introduced. The grass grows quite happily and the man-made reinforcing units help prevent it being worn away.

### LOW PLANTING
Car tyres can be catered for by providing firm standing on the two 'tracks', but plant low perennials and shrubs, such as thymes, ivies, helianthemums and other carpeters, in between for a softer look.

## Clothing the house

A climber or wall shrub works in partnership with the building it grows on, and each should complement the other. So, just as it's best to choose clothes that suit your particular colouring, it makes sense to select climbers that will go well with your walls. Complementary colours tend to work well together, and dark flowers against a pale background or vice versa. A blue clematis on a cream wall looks lovely, for example, while a shocking-pink rose or a red clematis against red brick is at best a wasted opportunity. Here are some ideas for climbers and wall plants that will make your house look classy:

### AGAINST RED BRICK
**Shade**  *Clematis* 'Marie Boisselot'; *Euonymus fortunei* 'Silver Queen'; x *Fatshedera lizei*

**Semi-shade**  *Clematis* 'Wedding Day'; *Hedera canariensis* 'Gloire de Marengo'; *Lonicera periclymenum* 'Graham Thomas'; *Rosa* 'The Generous Gardener'

**Sun**  *Abeliophyllum distichum; Abutilon vitifolium* 'Tennant's White'; *Myrtus communis*

### AGAINST STONEWORK
**Shade**  *Hedera helix* 'Parsley Crested'; *Parthenocissus henryana*

**Semi-shade**  *Clematis* 'Polish Spirit'; *Cotoneaster horizontalis; Rosa* 'Danse du Feu'

**Sun**  *Actinidia kolomikta; Campsis* x *tagliabuana; Ceanothus* 'Concha'; *Itea ilicifolia*

### AGAINST CREAM OR WHITE RENDER
**Shade**  *Garrya elliptica; Rosa* 'Tess of the d'Urbervilles'

**Semi-shade**  *Clematis* 'Frances Rivis'; *Hedera algeriensis* 'Ravensholst'; *Lonicera* 'Firecracker'; *Ribes speciosum; Rosa* 'Parkdirektor Riggers'

**Sun**  *Ficus carica; Vitis vinifera* 'Purpurea'; *Tropaeolum speciosum*

### AGAINST DARK WEATHERBOARDING
**Shade**  *Humulus lupulus* 'Aureus'; *Hydrangea anomala* subsp. *petiolaris*

**Semi-shade** *Chaenomeles* x *superba* 'Crimson and Gold'; *Pyracantha* 'Saphyr Jaune'; *Rosa* 'The Pilgrim'

**Sun**  *Clematis tangutica; Parthenocissus tricuspidata; Rosa* 'Climbing Iceberg'; *Rosa* 'Félicité Perpétue'; *Trachelospermum jasminoides; Wisteria sinensis*

# Contemporary gardens

The ongoing rejuvenation of many inner city areas has helped stir up a lot of interest in the design of contemporary small gardens. Outdoor spaces such as enclosed courtyards and roof gardens are a good starting point for creating clean-lined, modern outdoor rooms that don't need to worry too much about blending in with their wider setting. But when it comes to the planting in such intimate spaces, you'll realize there's nowhere to hide your mistakes – so you need to make sure everything is spot on.

Sustainable local materials and drought-resistant planting – topical themes in this 2005 Chelsea Flower Show courtyard garden, by staff and students of Chichester College.

## Materials and plants

A contemporary look requires a clutter-free space with plenty of light. This applies no matter how big or small the garden, though contemporary design is particularly effective in making small spaces look and feel bigger (see also pages 78–9). Consider pale-coloured or reflective construction materials: metal, glass, ceramic, perhaps set off by colour-washed walls. Garden furniture should be well designed, almost sculptural, and planting will probably need to be fairly minimal and architectural (see box). Plants with strong shapes, such as those with spiky foliage, are well suited to contemporary gardens. Grasses really come into their own – there are so many different ones available nowadays. Plant colours used in contemporary schemes are often cool, with strong contrasts: moody blackish purple with lime green, for example. White and silver are effective, too, looking very chic against a dark background or in the shade. Feed, water, weed and dead-head regularly: plants need to be in tip-top condition for the crisp, clean look you're after.

### Plant ideas for contemporary schemes

*Allium hollandicum*
*Cordyline australis*
*Eryngium giganteum*
*Euphorbia characias* subsp. *wulfenii*
*Fargesia nitida*
*Fatsia japonica*
*Hakonechloa macra* 'Aureola'
*Helictotrichon sempervirens*
*Hosta sieboldiana*
*Iris pallida* 'Variegata'
*Phormium* 'Maori Queen'
*Santolina chamaecyparissus* 'Lemon Queen'
*Sedum spectabile* 'Iceberg'
*Sempervivum tectorum* 'Atrorubens'
*Sisyrinchium striatum*
*Stipa gigantea*
*Yucca filamentosa* 'Bright Edge'

A detail of a Chelsea garden by Kate Gould, using materials favoured in contemporary design: brushed steel, decking and the tough perennial sedge *Carex buchananii*.

# Roof gardens

Roof gardens aren't new by any means, but increasingly they are being seen as a practical option by city dwellers; in fact, a roof garden may be your only option if you live in an upstairs flat. But first, make quite sure that it will be structurally sound. It may be necessary to strengthen the existing building to take the load, so consult a structural engineer before you even think about creating a roof garden. If it works, you will have the benefit of views to die for, as well as great light and a curious sense of seclusion that ground-hugging gardens can't match. All this lends itself well to a contemporary design.

Wind is sure to be a challenge, and you will need to create shelter and shade. Construction materials need to be chosen with the location in mind. A purpose-made roof garden on a new building may have solid walls for shelter, but this may not be the case if you are adapting an existing structure. Soundly fixed trellis is light and will filter the wind, and decking is often a good choice of flooring (*see* pages 45, 64–5).

Choose plants that can withstand regular buffetings. Think drought-tolerant, too. Those winds will dry plants very rapidly, especially if there isn't much depth of soil, and access for watering may not be easy. So build your scheme around undemanding plants: succulents such as sedums and sempervivums, low shrubs with felted or leathery leaves and tough, wiry grasses. Sheltered corners are ideal for sun-trap seating, and for tubs of dwarf spring bulbs and seasonal colour.

## 'Black' plants

Perhaps more than any other colour, black (or at least very dark) plants – sought after by nurserymen and gardeners alike – are particularly effective in a contemporary setting. Here are some favourites:

*Aeonium* 'Zwartkop'
*Alcea rosea* 'Nigra'
*Anthriscus sylvestris* 'Ravenswing'
*Euphorbia* 'Blackbird'
*Geranium pratense* 'Black Beauty'
*Helleborus* (many dark forms available)
*Hermodactylus tuberosus*
*Ophiopogon planiscapus* 'Nigrescens'
*Phormium* 'Platt's Black'
*Phyllostachys nigra*
*Pittosporum tenuifolium* 'Tom Thumb'
*Sambucus nigra* 'Gerda' ('Black Beauty')
*Scabiosa atropurpurea* 'Chile Black'
*Tulipa* 'Queen of Night'
*Veratrum nigrum*
*Viola riviniana* Purpurea Group

## Seeking inspiration

Visiting one of the growing number of annual flower shows staged in various parts of the UK from spring to autumn is undoubtedly the best way to sample contemporary design and planting ideas, ranging from the down-to-earth and practical to the way-out and wacky. The key events are organized by the Royal Horticultural Society (RHS), which awards medals to nursery exhibits and display gardens that are constructed specially for the show. Many of the show gardens are small, and special categories such as urban gardens and courtyard gardens are chosen for their practical relevance to garden owners. Make notes, take photos and talk to the exhibitors, who are usually on hand and only too willing to share their ideas and tips. Good shows to visit (most of them are also televised) include:

■ RHS Spring Flower Show (Cardiff, April)
■ RHS Chelsea Flower Show (London, May)
■ BBC Gardeners' World Live (Birmingham, June)
■ RHS Hampton Court Palace Flower Show (Surrey, July)
■ RHS Flower Show at Tatton Park (Cheshire, July)
■ RHS Flower Show at Malvern Autumn Show (Worcestershire, September)

Clean lines, stark colours and minimal planting are typical of many contemporary schemes. In this one by Diarmuid Gavin, a similarly styled roof terrace overlooks the oval deck.

# Cottage gardens

Garden fashions come and go, but the cottage garden seems to be a true perennial. With its luxuriance and its wide range of plants, this is a style that lends itself to the British climate and temperament. Although the exuberant planting scheme of a typical garden may look artless, its success will depend on choosing the right plants and exercising a little restraint.

Unpretentious yet dramatic, oriental poppies suit cottage gardens well. They need space, but cut them down after flowering and plant summer annuals around their crowns.

## Controlled exuberance

The most successful cottage gardens do have an underlying structure, however discreet. The hand of restraint may not be obvious, and the effect is probably better if it isn't, but it needs to be there all the same, to prevent the plants from engulfing one another and to provide some contrast to the luxuriance, so it doesn't all seem indigestible. Anything harsh, modern or clumsy is out, but limited areas of open space – such as paving or soft paths – are necessary to set off the billowing planting and invite you to wander through it, while hedges and fences, or perhaps some topiary, will create a contrasting backdrop. These structural elements help to hold the garden together and extend the season of interest so there is something to enjoy in winter, when the flowers have faded.

## Cottage gardens through time

Certain key elements of the traditional cottage garden style fit in well with today's enthusiasm for sustainable gardening. Keeping the ground densely covered with plants helps to save both work and water, since weeds are suppressed and evaporation is reduced. Mingling flowers with vegetables, fruit and herbs (*see* pages 106–9) looks good and helps foil pests and diseases, while self-sufficiency – an idea born out of necessity in times past – is now finding favour again. Cottagers were great recyclers,

Self-sowing flowers such as aquilegias and forget-me-nots are invaluable in cottage borders – especially (as here at Eastgrove Cottage) in spring, before roses take centre stage.

finding decorative garden uses for household cast-offs and reusing building materials such as bricks, chimney pots and roof tiles for different purposes. Other materials would have been locally sourced: sustainable hazel or willow for wigwams and plant supports, perhaps, and hurdles for fencing and gates, or for edging beds. Willow and hazel hurdles have become popular again today, and can even be fixed to an existing close-boarded or panel fence to fit in with the cottage garden style. Choose garden furniture carefully so it doesn't spoil the effect: rustic, antique or simple bistro-style tables and chairs would be good choices.

## Cottage garden planting

As to plants, the popular perception of a cottage garden is that anything goes, but the overall effect will be much more successful with a little discreet planning. As you head for yet another nursery, keep a few design principles in mind. Select some backbone plants – evergreens like holly, yew or santolina as well as strongly shaped perennials (alliums, eryngiums, irises) to add structure and texture and keep interest going through the seasons. If there's room for a tree, you may want an apple, with a clematis to climb through it, or a plum. You'll probably want plenty of 'old-fashioned' plants in the borders – perhaps aquilegias, foxgloves, hollyhocks, poppies, violas, pinks, wallflowers, sweet peas, lavender, honeysuckle ... the list goes on. Plants that self-seed (*see* 'Volunteers', right) encapsulate the spirit of cottage gardening and help

lend coherence to the planting scheme, often positioning themselves in just the right place. Whatever you choose, the overall impression should be artless – no matter how much forethought and effort have gone into achieving it.

There's nothing quite like sweet peas, one of the old-fashioned hallmarks of cottage gardening. Build a rustic structure of poles to support them and give height to the garden.

# Wildlife gardens

Garden design entails creating a whole environment. This involves not just the look of a garden but the life and movement that help make it a special place to be. Anyone who has a garden rich in wildlife will tell you that the creatures give them at least as much pleasure throughout the year as the plants. Watching your 'own' little ecosystem on a daily basis gives you an intimate knowledge and understanding of a host of fascinating lives and life-cycles, together with a constant sense of wonderment.

Foxgloves are ideal for a wildlife garden. They take over in early summer, when the profusion of spring flowers has come to an end, and if they are happy they will self-seed, increasing the size of colony year on year. Bees love them, too.

## Designing for wildlife

First, there's no need to transform your garden into a wilderness, nor to fill it with native plants. Ordinary gardens with ordinary planting can attract a whole range of wildlife with great success, provided of course that food chains aren't interrupted by the use of pesticides such as sprays and slug pellets. Habitats, too, must be preserved and not destroyed by over-zealous trimming, strimming and obsessive tidiness – particularly in spring and summer. Good design and wildlife gardening aren't in the least incompatible, and the usual principles still apply – from creating focal points to balancing planted areas with open spaces, or choosing a mixture of plant shapes and types for interest in different seasons. There are, though, a few key features that will make a real difference to the balance of wildlife in your garden.

## Planting for wildlife

Shelter and natural food for your wild guests should be your first priority. Hedges, trees and shrubs, including some evergreens for winter cover, provide not only places to hide and build nests, but also food in the shape of small insects and caterpillars, as well as winter berries. Include some native plants if you can. Many native trees, such as oak and ash, are too vigorous for the average garden, but hawthorn, birch, crab-apple and rowan are easier to accommodate, and are all attractive garden trees in their own right. Delay cutting down herbaceous plants until early spring and you may notice that in winter they attract seed-eaters, including goldfinches and chaffinches, as well as dunnocks, tits and wrens searching among them for tiny insects. Blackbirds and thrushes will keep you entertained with their enthusiastic rummaging among the dead leaves.

Boosting your garden's insect population by introducing a good mixture of different plants can be beneficial all round. With luck you will attract pest-eating predators such as hoverflies, ladybirds, spiders, lacewings and ground beetles. They are fascinating to watch at close quarters as well as being valuable gardening allies, helping to control aphids, slugs and many other pests. Open-centred flowers such as poppies, evening primroses and poached-egg flowers are good for hoverflies, while bees delight in catmint, foxgloves, eryngiums, sedums and many herbs such as thyme, mint, lavender and hyssop. Butterflies and moths use a huge range of plants as food for caterpillars or a nectar source for adults on the wing. Try *Centranthus ruber* (red valerian), *Sedum spectabile* (ice-plant), buddleia and *Verbena bonariensis*.

## Wildlife and water

A pond (*see* pages 72–7) is a magnet for all kinds of wildlife, attracting not only breeding frogs and other amphibians but also birds in search of a drink, or a plumage-restoring bath, or mud to help build their nests. Other visitors are likely to include hedgehogs and other small mammals, as well as bees and many different insects, among them several glamorous species of dragonfly and damselfly.

Another feature that will boost your garden's wildlife potential is the compost heap, a favourite hideout for centipedes, voles and the slug-eating slow-worm. Piles of logs, sticks or stones tucked under a shady hedge encourage newts, frogs and toads to lurk, and will also attract beetles, woodlice and other garden-friendly invertebrates.

A pond doesn't need to be huge or deep to make all the difference to garden wildlife, but it does need a gently sloping edge for access.

## Ten shrubs for wildlife

*Buddleja* (butterfly bush)
*Cotoneaster*
*Euonymus europaeus* (spindle)
*Hedera* (ivy)
*Hippophae rhamnoides* (sea buckthorn)
*Ilex* (holly – species and varieties)
*Prunus spinosa* (blackthorn)
*Pyracantha* (firethorn)
*Rosa rugosa* (Ramana rose)
*Viburnum opulus* (guelder rose)

The outsize hips of *Rosa rugosa* – a feast for the human eye and, in hard weather, for fruit-eating birds.

Positioning a birdbox high up a tree, but with easy access so you can clean it, will give nesting birds some protection from predatory cats.

Planting generous drifts of nectar-rich plants (here, Michaelmas daisies) will help butterflies find their way to your garden.

# Family gardens

A family garden is all about having something for everyone – easy to achieve if you have lots of space, but harder in a small town garden. A patio (*see* page 45), a lawn, a child-sized gardening area and a couple of well-designed pieces of outdoor play equipment form a good basis for a variety of outdoor pastimes, but the possibilities are endless.

Willow is a wonderfully easy, cheap and eco-friendly material for play structures such as a tunnel or a den like this. And building them is part of the fun, whether you're seven or 70.

## Lawns

Not every garden needs a lawn (*see* pages 70–1), but if you have a young family it is likely to be a priority. As a versatile, soft-surfaced open space for play and relaxation, lawns are hard to beat. You don't want a bowling green, just a tough grass mixture that can take a lot of punishment. (If you're starting from scratch, buy a special, hard-wearing grass-seed mix.) Don't cut the grass too short or you might end up with bare patches, especially in areas of heavy wear.

## Gardening with children

Lots of young children find great delight in gardening and the magic of making things grow. Children can

### Growing organically

Many parents now choose to garden organically. As well as producing chemical-free food, this eliminates the risk of children coming into contact with potentially harmful substances such as pesticides and weedkillers.

be involved in the planning and building of a specially designed little garden of their own, where they can grow plants that produce quick results. A timber raised bed, narrow enough for short arms to reach from both sides, is simple to construct (*see* page 43). If you edge it with stout planks nailed or screwed to posts sunk into the ground it should last as long as it needs to, and will give a lot of pleasure. A semi-shaded spot could be used for a small, acrylic-glazed cold frame, where seeds can be sown and cuttings rooted. And paths surfaced with chipped bark, with a seat and small table nearby, will finish it off nicely.

## Play equipment

A vast selection of play equipment made from natural materials is now available and will look far better in a garden setting than brightly coloured plastic, which never seems to mellow and can be hard to dispose of sustainably when no longer needed. You could of course

### Swimming pools

In hot weather what could be more perfect than your own swimming pool, but the design challenge is how to incorporate it without letting such a large feature dominate the garden. If you have the space, a separate, hedged enclosure is probably the best solution, ideally free from overhanging trees that will drop leaves into the water. You can plant the area exclusively for seasonal summer colour and fragrance to enjoy while you're using the pool, and forget about it for the rest of the year.

There are, however, other ways for swimming and gardening to go hand in hand. A good swimming pool installer with a little imagination should be able to offer you a tailor-made, harmonious design that is more garden-friendly than the standard bright blue rectangular box. An exciting new development is the 'swimming pond', a pool that looks and behaves like a natural pond. Aquatic plants chosen specifically to keep the water clean naturally, without the need for chemicals, are planted around the shallow margins, and there is a deeper, central area of open water for swimming. These ponds are a specialist construction job, but several companies in the UK now operate in this field.

spend thousands on a bespoke tree house or a sophisticated climbing frame, but children will have just as much fun, at a fraction of the cost, with a tunnel created from slips of living willow, a worn-out rowing boat picked up second-hand, or a sandpit made from a circle of logs set vertically into the ground or from a cleaned-up tractor or lorry tyre.

## Planting for a young family

Your garden may have to cater for budding footballers and games of hide-and-seek, but that doesn't mean plants are doomed. Choice, delicate specimens may have to wait a few years, but there are hundreds of attractive shrubs and perennials for which a few knocks are all in a day's work. Don't expect miracles – any plant deserves a bit of respect, after all – but try some of these:

*Ajuga reptans* 'Catlin's Giant'
*Alchemilla mollis*
*Buxus sempervirens* 'Elegantissima'
*Carex oshimensis* 'Evergold'
*Chaenomeles* x *superba* 'Crimson and Gold'
*Cornus alba* 'Elegantissima'
*Cotoneaster horizontalis*
*Euonymus fortunei* 'Emerald 'n' Gold'
*Geranium* x *magnificum*
*Ilex* x *altaclerensis* 'Golden King'
*Jasminum nudiflorum*
*Jasminum officinale*
*Lonicera nitida* 'Baggesen's Gold'
*Origanum vulgare* 'Aureum'
*Phlomis fruticosa*
*Rosmarinus officinalis*
*Sarcococca confusa*
*Tellima grandiflora* Rubra Group
*Thymus citriodorus*
*Verbena bonariensis*
*Vinca minor* 'La Grave'

Football needn't make your garden an eyesore. Designer Cleve West's goal is imaginatively created from sustainable materials – an attractive feature, yet practical and robust.

*Cotoneaster horizontalis* – an undemanding shrub that looks presentable all year and makes a useful filler for a family garden. Birds will enjoy the berries in winter, too.

### Don't forget

Water and safety are key considerations in a family garden. With very small children, even shallow open water is a potential hazard. Unless you want to go to the expense of covering it with a stout metal grille, it's best to wait until children are older before creating a pond of any depth. Some other kind of water feature, such as a fountain or bubble-jet pebble pool with an inaccessible, underground reservoir, would be much safer.

### Hazardous plants

An exhaustive list of garden plants that it's wise not to eat could fill a book. It goes without saying that children should be taught about the dangers as well as the pleasures of plants. There are a few common garden plants that look tempting but are dangerously poisonous if accidentally eaten, and others that commonly cause allergic skin reactions. You may prefer not to grow these until children are older:

| | |
|---|---|
| *Aconitum* | *Euphorbia* |
| *Arum* | *Ipomoea* |
| *Brugmansia* | *Laburnum* |
| *Colchicum* (below left) | (below right) |
| *Daphne* | *Ricinus* |
| *Digitalis* | *Ruta* |
| | *Taxus* |

# Formal gardens

The formal garden comes with an impeccable pedigree. Stately homes with parterres, balustraded terraces and billiard-table lawns spring to mind, but formality has a valuable role to play in many a more modest establishment. Often based on evergreen planting, the formal garden has year-round interest and can be low-maintenance. Some would say this style is more important than ever in the small, neat, town gardens that are features of many modern homes.

Symmetry and geometric shapes are critical to formal gardens but needn't look severe if combined with some informal planting – as in this 1997 Chelsea Flower Show garden designed by Xa Tollemache.

A geometric layout is what separates a traditional formal garden from the rest. Straight lines and right-angled corners are typical. Curves in the form of quarter- or semi-circles work well; other shapes may be acceptable if they are repeated symmetrically. Nothing should be free-form, abstract or (perish the thought) disorderly. The all-important architectural elements comprise good-quality, classic hard-landscaping materials (this goes for furniture and accessories too), and small-leaved evergreens – typically box or yew – clipped into wall-like hedges and topiary.

## Achieving a formal garden
Formality is tricky on slopes, so if your garden isn't level, do consider the landscaping implications before you plan a formal garden. Symmetrically laid out terraces, steps and paths will probably look fantastic when it's all finished, but make sure you are prepared for the expense and disruption that will be necessary to create that kind of garden. Even if no major earth-moving is involved, achieving the precision finish that a formal garden requires will need really meticulous attention to detail at every stage of planning and setting-out, to make sure that surfaces are level and smooth, angles precise and objects symmetrically positioned – and that's before you even begin to think about the planting.

## Maintenance
Think twice (at least) about your attitude to maintenance before launching into creating a formal garden. Even tiny lapses of attention are all too obvious in a garden of trim, straight lines and clean, flat surfaces. Lawns need to be in tip-top condition, gravel immaculately raked, and hedges and other topiary perfectly and precisely manicured.

## Formal meets informal
Most of us probably wouldn't want an entirely formal garden, but whatever you do, don't dismiss formality altogether. Above all, it's a great foil for informality. You can create both formal and informal areas to give contrasts in mood between different parts of a garden; formality works wonderfully well closer to the house; informality at a distance. The great plantswoman and designer Gertrude Jekyll liked to plant informally within a formal

structure, often working in partnership with the architect Sir Edwin Lutyens to create gardens that became classic set pieces. But you don't need to have a grand garden to use their ideas. Jekyll's use of colour harmonies in planting, for example, can be adapted to smaller gardens, or even a single border.

Show gardens – for example the small gardens at the Chelsea Flower Show – often fit loose, romantic-style planting into strongly designed, highly structural hard landscaping. You can pick up all sorts of ideas from the ways in which different designers have adapted this approach. One thing they have in common is that formal elements, such as symmetrical paths and steps, and clipped evergreens, ensure that the garden always has something to hold it together, even in winter. But, at the same time, the shapes, textures and colours change dramatically with the seasons – a pleasure that isn't easy to achieve in a wholly formal garden.

## Seeking inspiration

Classic gardens to visit in the UK where you can see the formal and the informal working successfully together include the National Trust's Hidcote Manor Garden, in Gloucestershire, and the late Christopher Lloyd's garden, Great Dixter, in East Sussex. Hidcote is a collection of garden 'rooms', formal and informal, working together to create different moods and forming a harmonious and satisfying whole. Dixter has exuberant, informal planting of different kinds, all given structure by a formal framework of venerable old yew hedging. If you want to see aspects of seriously stylish formal gardening, visit Ham House in Richmond or Levens Hall in Cumbria.

Formal hedges should be dead straight. When clipping them, run a length of taut string between two canes as a guide to ensure a level top.

## Topiary

Topiary has never really gone out of fashion. It appeals both to the control-freak end of the designer spectrum, for its strong architectural shapes (as in clipped pyramids, spirals and 'lollipops'), and to the quirky end, where the sky's the limit. There are many famous and much-photographed examples: topiary teapots, snails and locomotives, even a hunt in full cry.

There is something very satisfying about creating your own topiary feature, however small, and it can have a useful role in almost any kind of garden. A simple, clipped box ball or cone in a carefully chosen container makes a great focal point in even a tiny space; several of them, set along a path, give rhythm and continuity to a design.

If you're new to topiary, you'll need a pair of good secateurs and some small, sharp, one-handed shears ('sheep-shears' are ideal). Start with simple shapes, and progress to more intricate forms as you get more confident. You can buy wire frames in many different shapes, to put over the plant as a guide to clip round as it grows. Be sure to keep the plants amply fed and watered: plants that are continually clipped (especially those in containers) need to replace lost nutrients if they are to stay well furnished with healthy greenery.

Formal and informal can make excellent partners. Use topiary to contrast with meadow planting (as at Great Dixter, above) or juxtapose clean, cool hard landscaping with a tumble of foliage such as the grass *Stipa tenuissima* (left).

**Planning for low maintenance**

For a lot of people, garden maintenance is a necessary evil. Even keen gardeners often dislike repetitive chores such as grass-cutting and hedge-clipping. But it's actually quite simple to turn the situation to advantage. Ask yourself which tasks you least enjoy, and then spend some time re-planning the garden to eliminate the drudgery and create low-maintenance features that you know you will enjoy. After all, a garden is meant to be a pleasure and not a burden. You'll be surprised how easy it is to say goodbye to garden features that you don't consider to be worth the trouble – and how much better you'll feel when you have a garden that is right for you.

## Lawns

The traditional view is that no garden is complete without a lawn (*see pages 70–1*), but looking after a lawn properly is actually quite hard work, especially in a small garden where it may get intensive wear. All that spiking, weeding, feeding and mowing

can be a thing of the past if you opt for a low-maintenance alternative – perhaps paving or gravel softened by a cushion of mat-forming plants.

## Hedges

Think seriously before replacing an existing hedge with fencing to save on maintenance. Hedges have so many advantages, to wildlife and the environment as well as to the look of your property. You could replace an existing, high-maintenance hedge of

privet, Leyland cypress or *Lonicera nitida*, which needs regular trimming to keep it neat, with a different hedging material. Some of the best native hedging shrubs, such as yew, holly and beech, are very long-lived and can be kept looking respectable with just one cut a year.

Beth Chatto's inspired gravel garden is densely planted to suppress weeds, needs no watering, and has no grass to mow – all excellent labour-saving tactics.

## Saving time and effort

There's a lot you can do to make the garden less physically strenuous to look after when your circumstances change. You might have taken on a very demanding job that leaves little time for gardening, or recently started a family. After retirement, too, the plan may be to spend more time in the garden but, ironically, that's just when the ground is beginning to seem a bit further away, or the watering can be a bit heavier. Whether you are trying to cheat the advancing years or have other reasons to avoid undue exertion, here are some ideas:

■ If you are a keen gardener, turn your attention to enjoying plants on a smaller scale. A greenhouse, an upright cold frame or a potting shed can open up pastimes such as growing from seed, propagating, or growing specialist plants such as dwarf bulbs, bonsai, cacti and succulents, or alpines.

■ Re-plan borders with layered planting, which will mean minimal digging and weeding. Create a tapestry of ground-cover plants with interesting foliage, interplanted with spring bulbs. Weave in some tall, easy perennials for summer colour and some shrubs to flower in spring or autumn. Include a few evergreens – invaluable for both ground cover and winter structure.

■ Review your tool shed. Today there are many easy-to-use tools on offer that are a real boon to people who need help with lifting, bending or gripping.

## Raised beds

Anyone who has gardened in raised beds will tell you how much easier they are to look after. Somehow the very idea of gardening in a confined space makes the whole business seem more manageable, and of course it's far easier if you don't have to bend double to reach your plants. Plants, too, like raised beds, as they don't have to compete against encroaching weeds or battle through compacted soil. You can plant more densely, and if the top of the bed is at a convenient height it will double as a seat, and a place to put your cup of tea.

## HOW TO build a raised bed

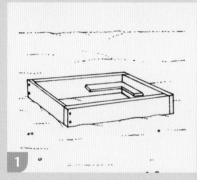

**1**

Cut four 150 x 50mm (6 x 2in) planks to the size and shape of bed you require. Screw them together, keeping the corners square, to create a frame. Cut four corner posts from 75 x 75mm (3 x 3in) timber. Their length should be the height of the bed plus 30cm (12in) to allow for sinking them into the ground.

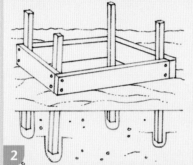

**2**

Use the frame to position the four corner posts, and dig post holes in the correct positions. Keep the posts upright, and sink them into the holes. For a small, temporary raised bed this should suffice, but larger, permanent structures will need the posts set in concrete (see page 63).

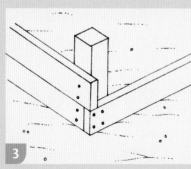

**3**

Build further layers of planks as in step 1 to the height of bed required. Screw the timbers to the posts as well as to each other, staggering the joints as shown.

**4**

Finish the top with a shelf made from the same planking, mitred at the corners and screwed to the posts. Add a 5cm (2in) layer of rubble or gravel to the bottom of the bed for drainage. Fill with a mixture of good topsoil and garden compost.

## Low-maintenance planting for containers

A group of thoughtfully arranged containers always makes a garden look well cared for, but it doesn't need to involve hours of work, or cost a fortune, if you choose the right plants. Start by building up a small 'background' collection of all-season, low-maintenance shrubs and other plants, bought in 2- or 3-litre pots and potted on into your chosen containers. Use a humus-rich compost or mix in a moisture-retaining gel, and add a slow-release fertilizer. That way, they will need repotting only once a year at most. Choose frost-resistant containers in a mixture of shapes and sizes. You can ring the changes by moving them around and adding a pot or two of seasonal colour, with bulbs or bedding plants for example, when you see something you fancy in the garden centre. Avoid being a slave to watering: choose relatively drought-tolerant plants, and don't let them become pot-bound or they will dry out very quickly. Keep them out of full sun in summer. Here are some to try:

EVERGREEN SHRUBS
*Buxus sempervirens* 'Elegantissima'; *Fatsia japonica*; *Gaultheria procumbens*; *Juniperus communis* 'Compressa'; *Osmanthus heterophyllus* 'Goshiki'; *Skimmia japonica* 'Rubella'.

GRASSES
*Carex buchananii*; *Festuca glauca*; *Stipa tenuissima*.

SUCCULENTS and 'EXOTICS'
*Cordyline australis*; *Phormium*; *Sedum*; *Sempervivum*.

Sempervivums are a great all-year standby, needing only good drainage.

# Hard landscaping

The term 'hard landscaping' is rather misleading. What it actually refers to is not just hard surfaces such as walls, patios and paving, but also gravel paths, water features, fences and other timber structures – in fact, everything except the planting. Some gardens get by without hard landscaping of any sort, and green initiatives of various kinds are encouraging us to manage with less of it. But there is no doubt that hard landscaping has practical advantages for year-round use as well as giving a garden shape and structure, and establishing boundaries for screening and security.

# Purpose and uses

Hard landscaping is usually the most expensive part of making a new garden, so think carefully about your choice of materials before you embark on costly practicalities. Built features that work well in relation to the surroundings of your plot, as well as complementing the house, will suit your garden best.

## Patios

The patio is a place to sit and unwind, and to entertain. It is where house meets garden and, if it's properly thought out and built – using sympathetic materials and appropriate planting – it will provide a strong link between the two.

When planning a patio, make sure it will be big enough to feel relaxed and comfortable. The cramped double row of slabs favoured by some house-builders is all but useless. You need room to move about as well as to sit, and some space for planting, in containers or in beds, with flowers spilling freely over the patio edges. Choose paving that suits the house, and consider how it will look and behave in the rain. Grey paving often looks depressing when wet, and smooth slabs can get very slippery. Think about drainage – always away from the house, please. Slabs in a mixture of sizes look less utilitarian (*see* page 58), and you may like to leave some of the joints unmortared so small plants can soften the effect.

## Decking

Decking has become hugely popular in recent years, but it is sometimes seen as the *bête noire* of contemporary garden design. True, it can look incongruous in the wrong place, but properly built decking offers a neat solution to many a design conundrum. It can be the answer to tricky problems with levels, and can be made to fit even the most awkward of shapes. It is ideal for providing a smooth transition from house to garden (*see* pages 64–5). Being lighter than paving, decking is especially useful where load-bearing is an issue, such as in roof gardens. Perhaps because of its nautical associations, decking and water are natural partners, so it lends itself to water features and

Decking and water – good companions, here looking rustic and artless as an alternative to the more usual chic and contemporary.

### Dining space

The patio is ideal for relaxed meals and barbecues with family and friends, so you need the right garden furniture. Obviously garden tables and chairs come in all shapes and sizes, but one thing they have in common is that they all take up more space than you think. You need room to push the chairs back, and for people to walk and stand about as well as to sit down. As a rough guide, you'll need a paved area of about 2.5 x 1.5m (8 x 5ft) to comfortably accommodate a table and chairs for two people, 3.5 x 3.5m (12 x 12ft) for a round table seating six, and 4.5 x 3.5m (15 x 12ft) for an oblong table to seat eight.

swimming pool surrounds. On the down side, decking is not very practical in shade, tending to become slippery when wet, and it's slow to dry out. You also need to think about the space underneath it, which can become a wasteland for rubbish and vermin.

### Don't forget

Check the origin of the timber for your deck, and make sure that it comes from a sustainable source (*see* page 57).

New hard landscaping looks a bit stark to begin with, but a season's growth and weathering will give everything the comfortable, established look you are after.

## Paths

Well-maintained grass paths look lovely, and grass is fine for paths that aren't used very often, but it won't stand up to a lot of wear. In wet weather it quickly turns into a mud-slide, especially on a slope. A hard-landscaped path may take time and trouble, but it will be more practical.

You'll probably have at least one main access route in the garden where you need a 'serious' path – solid, durable and probably made with mortared slabs, bricks or setts, properly laid on a firm foundation (*see* pages 58–9). But hard paths like this are too severe and formal for many situations, and it can be quite

a task to remove one if ever you want to change the layout. Often less ambitious paths will do nicely.

### Brick paths

Brick paths always look appealing, especially in informal gardens. There are any number of laying patterns to choose from – herringbone and basket-weave are two popular ones. Be sure to use frost-proof bricks. A mixture of slabs and bricks, or other contrasting materials like tiles, setts or slate, also works well; you can devise your own pattern. Paths using bricks can either be laid on a mortar base or in a more makeshift fashion on a bed of dry sand (though it's a good idea to have a mortared edging to prevent the bricks from creeping sideways). In unmortared paths you can grow little plants in the cracks, which looks charming, but the downside is you'll get plants you don't want, as well as those you do. Even if you put a geotextile membrane underneath, seeds of annual weeds will still find a home if the joints are not mortared.

### Less formal paths

There are many ways to make more informal paths. Laying slabs as stepping-stones is quick and easy. Set them into a bed of shingle or chippings, or simply into the soil for a path that crosses a flower border. Slabs as stepping-stones across grass

Slate chippings make an easy-to-lay informal path and are an effective foil for architectural plants, giving a rural but not an old-fashioned feel to this contemporary London garden.

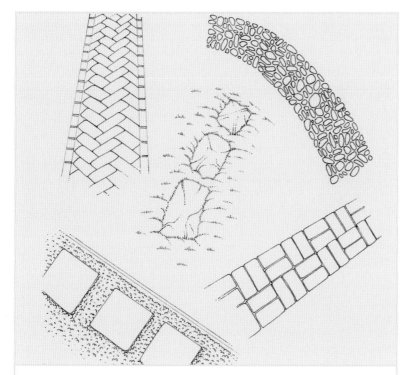

Brickwork patterns such as herringbone (top left) or basketweave (bottom right) are ideal for straight paths. Random-laid cobbles (top right) will fit any shape, while slabs in shingle (bottom left) or grass (centre) suit straight lines and curves.

Shingle and railway sleepers are an easy and well-tried solution where informal steps are needed. Planting will soon billow over the edges to give a softer effect.

are another option: lay them on a bed of sand or mortar to keep them stable, and recess them slightly below the level of the grass so the mower can pass over them.

Paths of loose aggregates such as pea-shingle, or chippings of limestone or slate, are easy to make, and ideal for irregular or informal shapes (see page 68). Chipped bark makes a good surface for a woodland-style path, but it will need topping up at intervals. It's best to edge this type of path with timber boards, bricks or a purpose-made edging such as twist-topped tiles, to stop the surfacing material from escaping at the edges. Loose aggregates, especially smooth, slippery pea-shingle, aren't suitable for slopes, although you can encourage them to stay put by making a series of shallow steps – using timber to contain the material.

## Steps

As with paths, there may be places where you need 'serious' steps and these should be solidly built, probably by a professional. Choose your materials with safety as well as appearance in mind, using non-slippery slabs or bricks for the treads and making all the steps the same height and width. A handrail may be worth considering, too. The odd step or two that may be needed along a path should be designed with a prominent edge so that you don't come upon it unawares.

You can be a bit more relaxed about decorative or casual steps, which can be built from logs, boards or railway sleepers, firmly fixed by means of sturdy pegs driven into the ground. The treads are then backfilled with earth or hard core and topped with a thin layer of aggregate such as stone chippings. Safety will still be important, so the steps should be of even height and not slippery when wet. Small-mesh galvanized wire netting can be stapled on to timber treads for grip.

Depending on what space is available, steps can either be set into a retaining wall or jut out from it, or they can be half and half. They can be parallel to the wall or at right-angles. And they don't have to be rectangular. Semicircular brick steps, if there is enough space, look particularly attractive.

If possible, avoid steep steps – like those that are normally used on an indoor staircase – anywhere in the garden. In an outdoor setting these feel cramped and too much like hard work. Garden steps feel more leisurely if they have deep treads of approximately 40–50cm (16–20in) and low risers of about 10–15cm (4–6in).

## Fences

With a little imagination, you can design and even build your own unique, bespoke fence, and garden boundaries might be a whole lot more interesting if more people did that. But if you have a new plot you will probably have other priorities and, at least in the short term, will want a standard, off-the-peg fence that can be put up quickly and without fuss.

A simple fence of posts and rails serves to mark a boundary, but most people want a fence to do other things besides, such as providing privacy and keeping the dog in. Below are some of the most popular fencing options.

### Panel fencing

Posts with prefabricated softwood panels between them make up this inexpensive type of fencing, which can be used to create a boundary of any height up to 1.8m (6ft). It is quick and easy to erect but not very durable, especially on windy sites. The panel infill – usually of larch, which is either woven or in overlapping strips – is very thin. Panel fencing doesn't suit steeply sloping sites because the panels must be horizontal, so erecting them on a slope leaves not only a stepped profile but also awkward triangular gaps, which will probably need to be filled, between the surface of the ground and the bottom of each panel.

Trellis panels are more attractive than solid ones, especially when clothed with climbing plants. Their open structure casts less shade, and filters the wind without causing turbulence, but it also means that they don't provide complete privacy. A happy compromise that can look really attractive, as long as it is well finished, is to use solid panels up to a certain height with trellis along the top. Ready-made trellis is available in different patterns and densities, and the tops of the panels can be concave, convex or wavy for a more decorative, undulating fence line. (*See also* pages 62–3.)

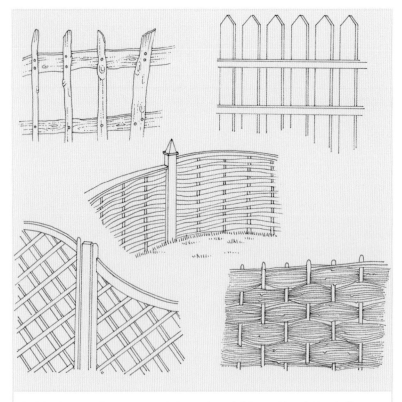

A picket fence can be custom-made from salvaged driftwood (top left) or built more conventionally (top right). Woven hardwood strips (centre) or willow wattles (bottom right) are better for screening, as is trellis (bottom left) when covered with climbers.

## Close-boarded fencing

This is a stouter and more costly type of fence. It is built on site by erecting concrete or timber posts at regular intervals, with two or more sets of horizontal wooden rails (called arris rails) between them, and then fixing overlapping feather-edged boards vertically to the rails. To make the fence more weatherproof, it is a good idea to protect the end-grain of the timber by fitting a narrow timber coping along the top.

## Openwork fences

Post-and-rail and post-and-wire fencing mark a boundary but don't function as an effective barrier for children or pets, nor do they give any screening. They are fairly cheap to erect, though, and can be useful for large rural gardens where you want to keep a view open and aren't concerned about privacy. Chain-link fencing is an efficient if not very attractive means of keeping dogs, livestock and children in (or out!). Flexible galvanized or plastic-coated wire netting is another option, fixed to stout posts, with straining wires to keep it in place.

## Traditionally crafted fencing

Traditional chestnut paling consists of lengths of split chestnut strung together with taut twisted wire. It is easy to erect and rustic-looking. Equally traditional, and often associated with cottage gardens, is picket fencing, which can be very attractive to look at but is quite fiddly to build. It is usually made of softwood, either treated or painted; white is the classic cottage colour,

but it will need regular maintenance to keep it looking smart. Wattle hurdles, once used for sheepfolds, are the product of another old country craft and are popular in cottage-style gardens. The panels are made of woven willow or split hazel rods. Hurdles look charming and rustic but do not last many years. To make them more durable, paint them every year with a mixture of linseed oil and turpentine, and check regularly to make sure the posts are rigid. You should do this because with age the panels become brittle and don't flex with the wind.

Railings and estate fencing are a different kind of traditional, but always have a certain cachet, in town or country. If you inherit this style of fence you will probably want to look after it as an asset to your property; it looks timeless and classy if kept smartly painted. Having iron fencing made to measure, from scratch, will be expensive, but it may be exactly what is needed to complement the garden and house, in which case it's money well spent – and it should last a lifetime.

## Gates

A garden gate can be anything from a practical, heavy-duty barrier whose sole function is to keep out intruders, to a highly personalized and decorative design statement, in either wood or metal. A gate is a natural focal point, and it's well worth a little extra trouble and expense to have one that looks welcoming and inviting, as well as complementing the style of your house and garden. If you have a gate made to your own design, whether

A hand-crafted ironwork gate makes a pretty but practical feature for a traditional garden. You may be able to design one yourself and find a local blacksmith to make it.

### Width of gateways

Make quite sure that gateways are wide enough for their intended use. For car access you need at least 2.4m (8ft) clearance between the gateposts, but even that will not accommodate a large delivery van.

The bare minimum for a pedestrian gate is about 60cm (2ft), but this is narrower than a standard interior door, and for a practical access gate you should allow 1–1.2m (3–4ft), which gives a bit more elbow room as well as access for a wheelbarrow, lawnmower, pram, wheelchair or bicycle.

it is solid or a picket style, always ensure that it is sufficiently well braced for its structure to hold its weight when hung in position. Traditional five-bar gates are usually designed with strong diagonal struts for just that reason.

## Arches, arbours and pergolas

These significant garden features are usually built of timber or metal and support climbing plants. An arbour is a small shelter for a seat; pergolas were originally walkways, but nowadays the term is also often used of a structure that shades an eating area (*see also* page 104). All need to be strongly constructed to withstand a fair amount of weight: a mature climbing rose or a wisteria in full flower can be pretty hefty. High winds are another hazard to factor in. Some cheaper, ready-made arches, arbours and pergolas are flimsy, while at the top end of the market prices can be astronomical. For something durable and cost-effective, it is often better to have it made by a local craftsman – or make it yourself (*see pages 66–7*). Use pressure-treated timber, and be sure the posts are securely concreted into the ground and that load-bearing components are up to the job.

## Gazebos, sheds and summerhouses

A roofed garden building can be as simple or as posh as you like, and it's

Make sure even a short-lived rustic pergola is designed and built to be sturdy enough to take the weight of vigorous climbers, such as this 'American Pillar' rose and accompanying honeysuckle.

*Clematis montana* var. *wilsonii* – charming cover for a rustic archway.

The perfect summerhouse – well sited, attractive and utterly inviting.

a great way of making more living space, and of extending the house into the garden. Whether yours is a tiny potting shed, a storybook tree-house retreat, a summerhouse or gazebo, or a fully fitted home office, remember that its bulk is sure to make it a focal point whether you like it or not. So either you must make it look devastatingly good or you must try to disguise it. You can hide a structure with planting, or lessen its impact by positioning it cleverly or painting it black to make it less obvious.

As with arbours and arches, an off-the-peg building is your least expensive option, but the quality and appearance may not be all you would wish for. If your budget permits, it may be worth spending a bit more and finding a local carpenter who could make you a bespoke building of better quality.

Alternatively, look for a second-hand structure that you can renovate. Architectural salvage companies and the local paper are good hunting grounds, or you may find just the right thing online. Before you buy, do check whether planning permission is necessary.

Positioning a large structure in an existing garden can be problematic. There needs to be enough working space to build a solid base for it, and it should be sited away from trees to prevent damage to their roots. Even the most attractive building may not look good stuck right in the middle of the garden, so be sure to give your structure a setting. Make it an attractive feature that is an integral part of the garden and it will be worth every penny.

## Siting a greenhouse

Choosing the right spot for a greenhouse isn't easy, but you'll be glad you took the trouble to find that spot *before* you put it up, rather than a couple of seasons later. Like other garden buildings, greenhouses seem to draw attention to themselves, and having one as a main focal point of your garden isn't necessarily what you want, unless you go for one of the more decorative models – but they don't come cheap. There's shelter to consider, too: you may avoid a bill for gale damage if you choose a spot out of the wind. Then there are the plants to think about; they won't want to fry all day in the heat of summer, but deep shade isn't what they need in winter. The site should be convenient for you, too, with hard paths to keep feet dry. A greenhouse that's a bother to trek to in winter is likely to be neglected. It's worth having water and electricity available. Using a paraffin stove may seem a handy idea until you find yourself going out in your pyjamas to light it at 2am.

A south-east facing position, where the greenhouse will catch the sun in the morning but not after midday, is often a good idea. The air inside will warm up quickly but gently as the sun strengthens, staying warm after it has gone, but the plants won't sizzle in the afternoon heat. Deciduous trees to the south of the greenhouse also work well, letting in plenty of light during the winter, when the plants need as much sun as they can get. The trees come into leaf just when the greenhouse is beginning to gasp a bit in the midday sunshine, and provide welcome shade through the warmest months. But don't let the trees overhang the glass or it will get covered in algae.

## Don't forget

When siting a greenhouse or garden structure, remember that you will need access all round the outside, for regular maintenance, repairs and glass cleaning.

# Hard landscaping materials

You only need to look at a few of the big garden shows, such as the RHS Chelsea Flower Show, to appreciate the bewildering range of hard landscaping materials now available. Even the choice of basics – bricks, paving, aggregates and timber – isn't straightforward. Arm yourself with as much background information as you can muster, and you'll have a much better idea of what to look for.

Brickwork is very adaptable in a garden – though it can be expensive.

## Bricks

There's no substitute for sympathetic landscaping brickwork to make a house and garden look as if they belong to each other. The ideal is to achieve a good match between the bricks used for each. But many ordinary clay bricks are not suitable for landscaping work because they absorb too much moisture when in constant contact with damp soil. When they become saturated, moss and algae can build up on the surface, and – worse still – frosty weather can make the bricks crumble. So before you buy bricks for paving, steps, edging or retaining walls, make sure they are frost-resistant. Special landscaping bricks are now available that are designed to blend with old brickwork, and some companies make clay bricks with a low enough absorbency for landscape use. So-called engineering bricks are the least absorbent of all; many of them are too utilitarian-looking for ornamental use, but some of the older ones can be quite attractive.

## Blocks

Concrete blocks, being much larger than bricks, are quicker and cheaper to build with, but are not objects of beauty and can really only be used where they won't be seen. They're fine for freestanding or retaining walls if the surface is going to be rendered, tiled or clad with a surface layer of stone or timber. You can also use them for building formal water features where they will be covered by a pond liner. The lightweight blocks used in house building may seem like an easy option, but they are for interior use and aren't really weatherproof or strong enough for most exterior hard landscaping jobs.

## Sand

You need different sands for different jobs. Building sand (or soft sand) is the cheap and cheerful orange stuff that you see lying around on building sites. It has fine particles and usually contains a small amount of clay, which makes it tend

A variety of hard landscaping materials are at work here, but they have been chosen and put together successfully to make a harmonious whole.

to stick together. It also stains hands, clothes and paving. It is used mainly for mortar where the colour is unimportant, and also for lining pond holes before the underlay and liner go in. Sharp sand (or grit sand) has larger particles and is used mainly as a bedding material for paving slabs. Silver sand is free-running and very pale, being almost pure silica. It is the best option for children's sandpits, and to fill the gaps between block paving. It's also useful, when planning, for marking out shapes on the ground by pouring it from a plastic bottle.

## Concrete

This is a mixture of cement with sand and coarse aggregate (the last two can be bought already mixed,

Classic hard landscaping gives definition to this garden and, though attractive in its own right, doesn't dominate the planting. The subtle patterns in the paving, and the strong lines of the seat and adjacent trellis, will help give the garden all-important structure in winter.

as all-in aggregate or 'ballast'). Adding water activates the cement to produce a compound that hardens quite quickly, strengthening as it dries over a period of days or weeks to form strong foundations and footings. The proportions of the ingredients vary according to what the concrete is to be used for, but for a general-purpose mix for small garden jobs use 5 or 6 parts pre-mixed ballast to 1 part cement. Laying large amounts of concrete is best left to the professionals, but for jobs such as setting fence posts or building a foundation for a small brickwork project (see pages 60–3), it isn't difficult to do it yourself, once you get the hang of achieving the right consistency, mixing the right quantity and getting the stuff into the right place before it sets.

Stone, clay or concrete setts are very versatile. Choose a laying pattern that echoes the lines of the garden.

## Concrete slabs

The easiest and cheapest kind of paving slabs are made from concrete. Many different products are available, ranging from the most basic square concrete slabs to paving that has been carefully moulded or tooled to look like real stone, available in a range of sizes to resemble random-cut flagstones. For circular or octagonal paved areas, or ones that include motifs or mosaics, you can buy special kits that contain all the right bits, so you don't have to cut awkward shapes. Thoughtful planning will also minimize the unpleasant job of cutting slabs. For example, make the width of a path an exact multiple of the width of the slabs you are using, if possible. (See page 58, Paving layouts.)

## Natural stone paving

Many kinds of local stone have traditionally been used very successfully for garden paving,

including sandstone, limestone, slate, marble and granite. Stone is still hard to beat as a classic natural material, but it is expensive to buy, as well as to cut and lay, and there are now growing worries about its environmental sustainability. Indian sandstone, and many other kinds of natural stone from overseas, have become widely available in recent years. They are a less costly alternative to locally quarried stone, but cheaper versions can be thin and uneven, needing extra careful cutting and laying. Some people prefer to avoid foreign-sourced stone on environmental or ethical grounds. Good reclaimed stone paving is often a successful (and greener) solution, and will add instant maturity to your garden.

## Reconstituted stone

Some companies specialize in making paving and other modular materials, as well as balustrading, fountains, planters and other garden ornaments, from a carefully blended mix of stone dust and cement. The result just about passes for stone but is less expensive than the real thing.

## Block paving and setts

Block paving has certainly improved since those uniform municipal-looking concrete blocks began to spread across driveways and car parks in the 1970s and 80s. Small-unit paving of this type, made from either concrete or clay, is available in different sizes and colours, with a worn or weathered finish to suggest old-fashioned cobbles. Properly laid, it can complement a house and garden well, and is a big visual

improvement on tarmac or concrete for front gardens – but 'properly laid' is the key. It must have a good, firm sub-base, especially if it is used by vehicles. Choose the material with care, and seriously consider getting it laid professionally.

Setts are small square units made from stone, clay or concrete, typically up to 100 x 100mm (4 x 4in) in size. They look good alongside slabs of a similar colour, and are ideal for durable, cottage-style paths. Some are available in larger square units with false joints, making them much quicker to lay. When pointed in, the real and the false joints look just the same.

## Gravel and chippings

Shingle – often called pea shingle – consists of small, smooth stones extracted from river or sea deposits.

It is usually available in two grades: up to 10mm (½in) or 20mm (¾in). It's clean and inexpensive, but the smoothness of the stone does mean that shingle moves around quite easily underfoot or beneath car wheels. Stone chippings, such as small pieces of quarried natural limestone, tend to be more angular and lock together to give a more stable surface. They come in many colours and rock types. Most often on sale are limestone, granite or slate, but with a little patience you can source almost any kind of rock you like. There are also various man-made granular materials, ranging from chopped-up, recycled tyres to coloured glass. Show gardens over the years have used some quite outlandish path surfaces, including one memorable path made out of rusty washers. Clearly the sky's the

Paving slabs needn't be boring. They can be combined with other materials, including grass, to make an attractive and unusual layout. The grass grid and square beds here will also help absorb rainwater and minimize run-off (*see* page 31).

## What lies beneath

Paving and driveways need a compacted sub-base to spread the load and prevent heavy weights from making hollows in the surface layer. For this you usually use either well-compacted hard core (waste broken bricks, concrete and so on) or a relatively cheap, coarse, crushed stone product that builders' merchants will deliver. This goes under different names but is often called 'scalpings'. It's a mixture of lumps (up to about 40mm/ 1½in in size) and dust, the idea being that the dust settles between the lumps to give a firm, stable base. The material is compacted with a 'whacker plate' or vibrating plate compactor. As a guide, a tonne of scalpings will cover about 5sq m (50sq ft) with a layer that is 100mm (4in) thick when compacted.

A perfect blend of rural and stylish. A stout, traditional post-and-rail fence of split chestnut is brought to life by a planting of white foxgloves, with cosmos in between to flower later.

limit, but for a real garden you have to bear in mind that some of these ideas are more practical than others.

## Timber

Wood is an ideal material for many garden structures, being versatile enough for anything from a railway sleeper to a feather-light batten. It is natural, relatively inexpensive, light, and easy to cut and shape. It is reasonably long-lasting, especially if given a little care to protect it from the worst effects of the weather. The woods from different trees vary hugely in their durability, so it's important to choose the right wood and to look after it, if it is to withstand rain and fend off the ever-present threat of fungal attack.

'Hardwood' generally means timber from broadleaved trees such as oak, ash or chestnut, while 'softwood' comes from conifers such as pine and larch. Hardwood timber normally lasts longer, but it's more expensive and more difficult to

work with. Softwood is often sold pressure-treated, which means it is impregnated with chemicals to make it last longer. In these days of vanishing rainforests, it's vital to make sure that all the timber you buy comes from environmentally responsible sources (*see* page 57).

### Posts

For most purposes – such as fences, trellis, light gates, pergolas and arches – standard fence posts in pressure-treated softwood will be fine for the uprights, which should be securely concreted into the ground (*see* pages 62–3). Choose posts measuring either 100 x 100mm (4 x 4in) or 75 x 75mm (3 x 3in) in section, weighing up the strength you need against the hefty appearance (and higher cost) of heavier posts.

A traditional option, if you prefer to avoid chemically treated timber, is to use hardwood posts such as oak. However, if you want to build a large oak structure such as a pergola or

arch it's wise to find a craftsman with traditional construction skills, who will make a structure that flexes, as green oak tends to move and twist as it matures.

### Railway sleepers

Timber doesn't come any sturdier than this. Sleepers are a quick yet durable fix for certain landscaping tasks, though you will need help to lay them as they are very heavy and difficult to cut. You can either stand them side by side, on end (sunk securely into the ground), or lay them horizontally, to make terraces and raised beds. Secure them together by drilling vertical holes to take steel reinforcing rods, which, in the case of horizontally stacked sleepers, can then be driven into the ground. Sleepers also make a good,

Timber sleepers set across a path give substance and emphasize width.

stout edging, especially for steps with treads surfaced with chipped bark or gravel (*see* page 47).

Ask your supplier whether their sleepers are new or recycled, where they have come from and whether or not they have been treated. Sleepers treated with recently outlawed preservatives such as old-style creosote should no longer be sold, and some kinds of preservative can ooze messily in hot weather. Untreated sleepers can be sourced, and you may prefer to specify these, particularly if you garden organically.

## Rustic poles

Ever popular rustic poles (usually larch) are cheap and very easy to work with, and they can be simply and quickly lashed or nailed

together to make arches, arbours and screens. The downside is that they are not at all durable, losing their bark and rotting at the base within only a few years.

If your garden is large enough to grow hazel or willow, you can have fun building short-lived structures such as rustic arches and obelisks from your own highly renewable coppice. Cut the trees almost to the ground, and within four or five years they will have produced a crop of usable, straight poles – all for free. The process will continue almost indefinitely, and you can use the twiggy growth as supports for rows of peas in your vegetable patch or for tall herbaceous plants in your borders, so they don't flop over.

## Board for outdoor use

Ordinary composite boards such as plywood, particleboard or MDF are not intended for outdoor work, and even so-called 'marine ply' can buckle and split if not protected.

## Trellis panels

Ready-made trellis panels from garden centres or builders' merchants come in a range of sizes up to 1.8m (6ft) high and wide, usually with a choice of square or diamond-shaped screen patterns. They tend to be rather thin and flimsy, but are handy for making a quick screen and will last longer if treated with preservative or painted. Well-made, more substantial and attractive trellis is available to order, at a price, from specialist companies. You may consider having it made locally or, alternatively, making it yourself using inexpensive battens.

### Environmentally responsible timber

Not so many years ago, strong and durable tropical hardwoods such as teak and mahogany were used with abandon for outdoor furniture, garden structures such as decking, and for just about anything else that needed to last a long time. But now, more people are becoming concerned about where their timber comes from and want to be reassured that their choice of pergola isn't helping to wreck the world's rainforests as well as the lives of the indigenous peoples who live there. Many garden products are now labelled as FSC (Forest Stewardship Council) certified. The FSC is an international body promoting sustainable management of forests. Their certification scheme means that we can all identify timber that meets certain internationally recognized environmental standards – so look out for the labels when you next shop for timber products.

Living willow is a fun material to work with, as well as being environmentally sound. It can be used to make screens and arches or, as here, a leafy rustic arbour that won't be quite like anyone else's.

# Hands on: Paving

Laying paving isn't rocket science, and with patience and a bit of careful planning the job should go smoothly and leave you with a patio or path to be proud of. The instructions here are for a basic paving job, but you can customize your paving with a contrasting edging or by replacing a few of the slabs with gravel, slate chippings or a different kind of hard surface such as bricks or granite setts. Small planted beds are another option. Browse through paving manufacturers' catalogues or look at websites for inspiration and ideas.

Letting plants colonize paving cracks creates a softer effect, but you have to keep on top of the weeds.

Once you've got the hang of laying standard paving, you can use your new-found skill to create custom-made paved areas that will set your garden apart from the rest. But do remember that the simplest schemes are often the most effective.

## Don't forget

Large paving slabs and bags of aggregate are very heavy and you could all too easily damage your back – even while unloading them from the boot of your car. Ask a helper to assist with lifting materials, and remember to let your knees rather than your back take the strain when lifting.

## Paving layouts

Uniform square slabs are straightforward to lay, and it's easy to work out how many you'll need, but this style of paving can look like a kitchen floor, only outside. Layouts using slabs of different sizes look better, suggesting traditional flagstones. Designing a bespoke layout before you start means that you can order exactly the right number of slabs of the various sizes and minimize any cutting of slabs. The snag is that it can take ages to work out a 'random' layout that will exactly fit your space, particularly if you are using a lot of different sizes.

Computer-aided design (CAD) is a great way to tackle this task and works like magic. You can find CAD services online that, for a fee, will generate custom-made laying patterns. For free help, contact paving manufacturers. Some publish plans for specific patio dimensions using their own products. If you'd rather do it yourself, get some squared paper and a pencil (and a good eraser!), draw everything to scale (1:50 or 1:100 work best) and prepare for a long session of fiddling around in order to get it right. If you colour-code each size of slab when you've finished, it will be easier to count up how many of each size you need to order. Don't forget to allow for 10mm-wide mortar joints.

## Drainage

Hard surfaces can't soak up rain like a lawn or a planted bed, so they need a slight slope to help shed water. Puddles and lingering dampness encourage slimy algae. Icy weather makes wet paving even more dangerous and can also make mortar joints crumble. As a rule of thumb, aim for a slope of between 1 in 50 and 1 in 100 – that's a fall of 1–2cm (½–¾in) in every metre (40in) of length. Rough surfaces such as riven paving should be at the steeper end of the scale, while smooth materials can have a shallower slope. Make sure the slope falls away from buildings and consider what is going to happen to the water after it runs off. For normal paths and small paved areas, drainage into an adjacent border will probably be fine – especially if your soil is light and drains well. For larger hard areas, or on heavier soils, you may need to plan for drainage into a purpose-built soakaway. Don't let surface water drain away into sewers, as this increases the risk of flooding in wet weather (see page 31).

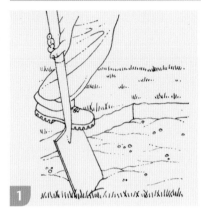

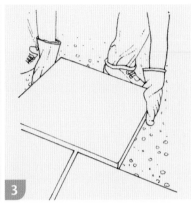

**1** Use pegs and string to mark out the area to be paved, then dig out the soil to a depth of about 20cm (8in) below the intended surface level. Don't disturb the soil below that. If the paving butts right up to the wall of the house, the finished surface should be at least 15cm (6in) below the existing damp-proof course and sloping slightly away from the house (*see* Drainage, opposite).

**2** When the shape is right, knock some levelling pegs into the ground, using a plank and a spirit level to check that they are at the right height – about 10cm (4in) below your intended surface level (the depth of the slab plus a mortar bed of 50–60mm (2–2½in). Then spread an even layer of scalpings across the area and use a powered compactor plate (available to hire) to firm it level with the pegs.

**3** If you have made a paving layout plan (*see* opposite) now's the time to test it out. (It takes serious determination to put mistakes right once the mortar has set.) So, lay out the slabs 'dry', in your chosen pattern, to check the fit and the look. Aim for a gap of 10mm (½in) between slabs. Make sure the edges align, slightly adjusting the width of the joints between slabs, if necessary, to achieve this.

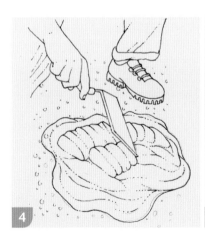

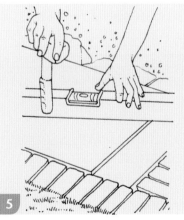

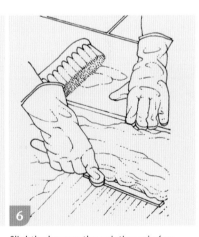

**4** Mix the mortar (*see* page 60). A small barrow-load at a time should be about the right quantity to mix so you can use it up before it sets. Make the mix quite sloppy. Lay slabs a few at a time, setting them to one side while you spread the mortar. The mortar layer should be about 50–60mm (2–2½in) deep. Use a trowel to make a ridged surface, which will help with levelling the slabs.

**5** Carefully lift the first paving slab into position. Rest it on the mortar bed and gently tap it level with the handle of a hammer. Check with a spirit level to make sure you've kept an even, very slight slope away from the house wall. Repeat with the other slabs. Don't walk on the slabs for at least 24 hours so the mortar can set properly. Over-eagerness can result in wobbly paving.

**6** Slightly dampen the pointing mix (*see* page 60) and fill the joints, pushing it in with a gloved hand and leaving no gaps or cracks. Finish the joints with a rounded stick or any similar tool that will give a neat, smooth finish. Sweep up any surplus mixture promptly so it doesn't stain the paving. The pointing mix will gradually absorb water from the ground and from rainfall, and will then set hard.

# Hands on: Brickwork

Bricklaying may look straightforward, but in reality it's a complex skill that takes a long time to learn. For an amateur it's much slower and trickier than you might think, and most jobs involving brickwork or blockwork are probably best left to a professional. All the same, there will be keen DIY enthusiasts who want to have a go, and it can be truly satisfying to know you've completed the task yourself – not to mention cheaper.

Before embarking on brickwork, there are quite a few decisions to be made. First you have to choose the right kind of bricks and think about the colour of the mortar and how much to make at once. Then you need to select the most suitable brickwork bond, pointing style and coping. Also ensure you take appropriate reinforcing and damp-proofing measures so that the finished wall will be sound, stable and safe. All this will be second nature to an experienced bricklayer, but a challenge for the novice.

### Make it simple

Start with a small project, such as a low wall or a brick edging for a path. The instructions opposite are for a single thickness of bricks ('half a brick thick'), in the basic 'stretcher bond' pattern, with bricks simply laid end to end. This is the simplest kind of wall, but suitable only for walls up to about 60cm (24in) tall, and not for a load-bearing or retaining wall. For a taller or more robust wall, you will need a double layer of bricks ('one brick thick'), using a stronger brickwork bond.

Brickwork and planting have a natural affinity, especially if mellow old bricks are used – and these tulips are the perfect complement.

## Copings

The top of a retaining wall or freestanding garden wall is usually finished off with a coping or cap to help prevent water getting into the top of the wall. Copings can incorporate a damp-proof course and they usually have an overhang to keep heavy rain off the sides of the wall, too.

You can buy purpose-made coping stones of various kinds, or why not try designing your own scheme using sloping tiles or slates (builders call these creasings). Look out for copings and creasings on old, traditional walls for inspiration – they often add a nice touch of individual decorative detail.

A simple and traditional capping for a wall that is one brick thick consists of a row of bricks set on edge. This works well with retaining walls, especially ones at 'perching height', for sitting on. A wall like this should be 55–60cm (22–24in) high, probably amounting to six courses plus a capping of bricks on edge.

A timber coping (below) won't be as durable as a brick one, but it can look attractive, is easy to fit and will be considerably less chilly to sit on than stone or brick.

## HOW TO lay bricks

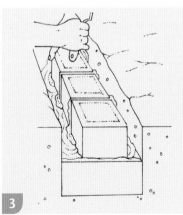

**1** Mark out a trench at least three times the width you want the finished wall to be, and dig out the soil to a depth of about 30cm (12in), keeping the topsoil separate. The base of the trench must be firm, so if the soil is soft, dig out some more and replace it with a layer of compacted hardcore or scalpings.

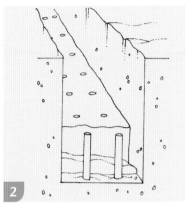

**2** Hammer some wooden pegs into the base of the trench, with their tops where you want the bottom of the wall to be. Check with a spirit level that the pegs are all at the same height. Then pour in concrete (mixed using 6:1 ballast : cement) up to the tops of the pegs and leave for several days to set.

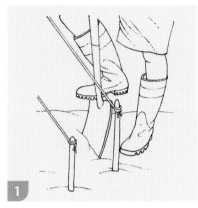

**3** Mix up some bricklaying mortar and spread a 10mm (½in) layer along the concrete to the required width. Lay the first brick, and use a spirit level to check for correct level and alignment. Then 'butter' the end of the second brick with mortar and butt it up to the first. As you lay, keep checking that each brick is horizontal and level. If a brick is too high, tap it gently with the trowel handle to level it. If it is too low, put more mortar underneath, then check again with the spirit level.

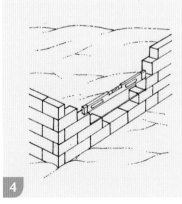

**4** Once the first course is laid, begin to build up the ends or corners, checking that each course is level and the sides are aligned. To stagger the joints correctly, start at one end of the second course with a brick set at right angles if you have a corner, or cut in half if your wall is straight. Fill in the courses between the corners or ends, checking that all is level and straight. A string line will make this easier. Keep mortar joints a constant width to ensure everything fits. Finally, smooth the joints and clean any mortar residue off the sides.

# Hands on: Posts and panel fencing

On reasonably level ground a panel fence is usually the easiest kind to put up. The same method can be used to erect trellis panels for screening, or it can be adapted for other types of fencing, or even for making a wooden compost bin. Concentrate on keeping the uprights vertical and on getting everything else straight, and you won't go far wrong.

Whatever kind of fencing you decide on, it will need posts, and so will a pergola, a deck and many another kind of garden structure. There's no great mystery to putting up posts, and it's a useful technique to learn and have under your belt. Once you've got the hang of it you'll be able to save a fortune in bills from fencing contractors. You'll also be half-way to building your own custom-made garden structures.

The step-by-step guidance opposite applies to timber posts (*see also* page 56). You can also buy concrete ones that have a groove to fit the panel into. This might sound easier but, while they last almost indefinitely, concrete posts are heavy and awkward to handle, they cost more and they don't do a great deal for the look of your garden.

It's easy to fit trellis to the top of a fence (see step 5, opposite), and it will improve screening without giving you that shut-in feeling or cutting out too much light.

Panels with curved tops look stylish. They can be used with success to end a run of trellis so that it doesn't come to an abrupt stop. Wooden finials give a neat finish.

## Timber preservatives and colours

Different timbers vary greatly in durability. Generally speaking, you don't need to treat hardwoods with any preservatives. Oak and tropical hardwoods such as teak, for example, can last for many years, weathering to a nice silvery finish that fits in very well with the planting. Various blended timber oils, such as teak oil and Danish oil, are available if you want to keep hardwood looking like new.

Softwood is another matter. Except for a few expensive timbers including western red cedar, untreated softwood is not durable enough for outdoor use. You can either buy it already pressure-treated or paint it with a preservative to help protect it from rot. Conventional coal-tar creosote was, until recently, widely used for treating fences and sheds, but safety concerns led to its withdrawal from general sale in the EU. A number of other chemicals (some of them highly toxic) that were formerly used freely in timber preservatives have also been replaced by safer alternatives. Even so, pressure-treated timber and commercial timber preservatives should never be used near water in case of contamination, and some people now choose to avoid them altogether, turning to alternative compounds using natural resins, vegetable oils and the less harmful inorganic chemicals such as borax.

The best 'green' advice is to buy good-quality timber, whether hardwood or softwood – sustainably sourced, of course (*see* page 57) – and to prolong its life by keeping it clean and free from algae, and by regular treatment with a low-impact product such as a vegetable-based oil.

Painting timber can help it to resist weather. There is a wide range of paints and woodstains for outdoor timber on the market, many of them much safer than their predecessors. They are available in many colours and very easy to apply.

## Don't forget

Both ends of the fence need posts, so you will need to add one more post to the number of panels you plan to buy.

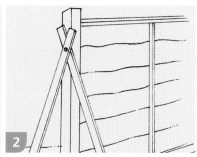

First mark out the position of the fence on the ground and calculate how many panels and posts you will need. The posts should be 75 x 75mm (3 x 3in) or 100 x 100mm (4 x 4in) in section, and one-third as long again as the final height of the fence. Dig the first post hole deep enough to allow one-quarter of the post to be sunk into the ground. Put in the post, check that it is perfectly vertical using a spirit level and then fill the hole almost to the top with concrete (1:6 cement : ballast). Pack the concrete down with a stout piece of wood.

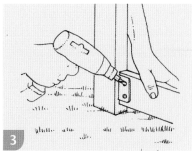

Brace the post temporarily with two timber battens, making sure that it doesn't move from the perpendicular. Leave it at least overnight for the concrete to set. You can now dig the other post holes. Use a piece of gravel board cut to the length of a panel to measure out their positions. (Don't forget to allow for the width of the post in between panels.) Next, set up a level string line to run from the first post, just above the height of the fence, to a temporary post or cane at the other end. The exact height isn't critical but it will help you to get the panels level.

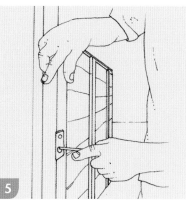

Cut a pressure-treated gravel board to exactly the same length as the panels. Fix it to the post with a U-shaped galvanized panel bracket, supporting the board from underneath to get it level and making sure the alignment is right. This is important because you will be using the gravel board as a base for the fence panel, so if the board is crooked, the fence will be too. If there's a gap between the board and the ground (as there will be if the fence is on ground with even a slight slope) you can fill it later with soil or stones.

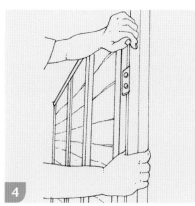

Fit two or three panel brackets, evenly spaced, to the first post, screwing in each one securely. Then perch the first panel on top of the gravel board. Ask a helper to hold it steady for you (especially if it's windy) while you screw the sides of each bracket into each side of the panel to attach the panel to the post. If the fence is on level ground, try to get the brackets at the same height along the whole length of the fence. This will give you a much neater effect.

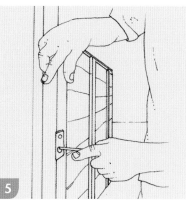

Set up the next post, checking the verticals. Fix it to the end of the fence panel and when everything is in place fill the hole with concrete as before. Continue fitting boards, panels and posts in this way until you reach the end. You may need to cut the last board and panel to make it fit the remaining space. If the fence is to be topped with trellis, fit this now by screwing each trellis panel to the posts at either end. Finally, fit post caps to protect the posts from rain.

There's always scope for customizing a plain fence. Decorative finials in various shapes and styles can be bought in do-it-yourself stores, or you may know a local craftsman who would make exactly what you want.

# Hands on: Decking

Decking is a good choice if you want to create a smooth transition from indoors to out, or from an elevated ground floor to a garden on a lower level. A new conservatory or garden building may have left you with awkward shapes and levels to deal with, or it may need a visual anchor to connect it with the garden. Decking is often the answer.

Decking may look complicated, but building it is easier than it might seem, though for large or high decks, or those spanning different levels, it may be a wise move to get professional help. The basic method outlined opposite could also be adapted to building a boardwalk or even a simple footbridge.

It's important to use the right materials. Structural timbers must be strong and durable while the deck itself must be weather-resistant and splinter-free. In wet weather, and especially in winter, decking can become slippery and can take time to dry out. Purpose-made grooved boards are fairly firm underfoot if

you keep them clean. They are widely available in softwoods such as cedar, as are handrails, posts and other accessories.

A deck can be very simple or as ambitious as this one, with changing levels, tailored planters and even a mature tree with a hammock to lie in.

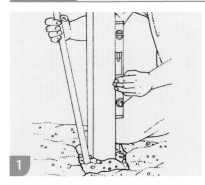

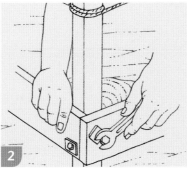

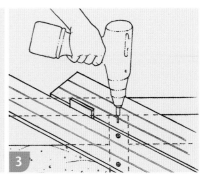

First erect the posts that will bear the framework. You'll need a pressure-treated 100mm x 100mm (4 x 4in) post at each corner and one about every 1.5m (5ft) around the edge of the deck. Level the ground and take out any large weeds and roots, but try not to loosen the soil too much. Dig a hole about 30 x 30 x 30cm (12 x 12 x 12in) for each post and lay half a concrete block flat on the bottom of each hole to spread the weight. Stand each post upright on its block and fill the hole with concrete, making sure the posts are perfectly perpendicular. Leave several days for the concrete to set properly. Cover the entire area to be decked with permeable black matting to keep weeds down, anchoring it with a covering of shingle.

Begin to build the framework of joists, using 150 x 50mm (6 x 2in) timbers cut to length. Start around the edges, fixing the joists to the outside faces of the corner posts with heavy-duty galvanized coach bolts (*see* Timber fixings, below). Check that these joists are level, then begin to fix other joists to them inside the framework at 45cm (18in) intervals. Use joist hangers (or other suitably strong metal fixings) and robust screws for this. Make sure the joists are parallel. Fix shorter pieces of timber ('noggins') between each pair of joists, at staggered intervals, to make the structure more stable. You can now cut off the posts to the required height – either flush with the joists or higher up if you want them to support a wooden rail or a rope barrier round the edge of the deck.

Build the surface of the deck with 100 x 25mm (4 x 1in) grooved boards. Start by positioning them across the framework. If the deck adjoins a building, they can be parallel to the wall, at right-angles to it or at 45 degrees to it. Leave 5mm (¼in) gaps between the boards to allow rainwater to run off. Push thin, evenly sized pieces of wood (spacers) in between the boards as you work to help keep the spaces constant and the boards parallel. Stagger any joints, and leave a generous overhang of at least 50mm (2in) around the edges. Now screw the boards to the joists, countersinking the screws so they don't stick up. Use a straight edge to draw a line around the edge of the deck and trim the boards so that they have the same overhang all the way round.

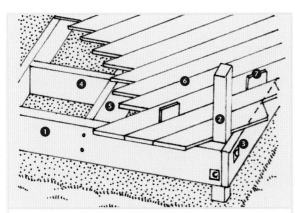

A corner of the completed decking, showing the framework of joists ①, a post ②, galvanized coach bolts ③, a joist ④, a noggin ⑤, decking boards ⑥ and spacers ⑦.

## Timber fixings

Any timberwork is only as strong as the joints and fixings that hold it together. For outdoor projects, especially, it's important to use accessories that are up to the job and that will withstand everything the weather can throw at them. Never use cheap, flimsy fixings, or ones that will rust easily, for load-bearing structures. This is a false economy and will cost you more in the long run. Screws, bolts and other fixings should be hot-dipped galvanized, or made from stainless steel, or brass. Solid brass is the best and most durable option for decking, but definitely more expensive. For joining heavy timbers in load-bearing frameworks, use coach bolts 10mm or 12mm in diameter. Ensure that they are long enough for the nut to be at least 5mm (¼in) from the end. Pre-drill screw holes, which will prevent the timber splitting. An exception to this is if you use special decking screws. These enable you to avoid the tedious job of pre-drilling holes when fitting deck boards.

For most jobs, screws are preferable to nails, which are quicker to fix but can work loose, bend, or split the timber. If you do use nails outdoors, make sure they are galvanized to help prevent failure or staining through rust.

# Hands on: Timber pergolas

Pergolas come in all sizes, shapes and materials, with their supporting uprights built of brick, stone, metal or timber. Some are a bit ambitious for an amateur DIY enthusiast, but with a little time, patience and a bit of basic know-how, building the framework of a simple timber pergola is not difficult. Your 'home-grown' pergola will probably be stronger and better value for money than a ready-made one that comes in kit form, and you can tailor the size and style to get exactly what you want.

Come into the garden … The pergola here transforms a shady passageway to make a leafy and inviting approach to a greenhouse.

A small freestanding pergola will need four uprights, one at each corner – size is a personal choice but don't make the posts too skimpy. Each pair supports a longitudinal beam, bolted to the uprights. The beams, in turn, support a series of evenly spaced joists, fixed to the beams by means of cross-halving joints. To make these, a rectangular notch is cut to half the depth of each timber, in the top of the beam and the bottom of the joist. The notches interlock at right angles, helping to make the structure more stable. The joists usually overhang the beams by 30cm (12in) or so, to give the pergola balance.

## Make a plan

Before you start, sketch a plan of the pergola, with measurements, and list the materials you will need.

Be sure to buy uprights that are long enough: 3m (10ft) sounds a lot, but is usually about right (unless the pergola is disproportionately narrow). This will allow plenty of height – about 2.4m (8ft) – for people and romantically dangling climbing plants, and still leave a 60cm (24in) length to bury in the ground as a firm anchor. The side beams and joists that make up the roof of a pergola, arbour or arch can be made with treated softwood measuring 150 or 200 x 50mm (6 or 8 x 2in) in section, cut about 60cm (24in) longer than the distance across the structure between posts, to allow for an overhang. This size of timber will provide a generous depth for notched joints and will be strong enough to withstand the weight of climbing plants.

## Pergolas on buildings

A pergola can make an attractive and practical addition to a house wall (ideally south-facing). Planted with deciduous climbers, this extra 'room' outside will be a pleasure to eat or relax in during the summer. It will also shade the windows in summer but let light into the house in winter. Assuming there is space on the wall, you'll need to adapt the basic timber pergola so that one side of it is supported on the house wall rather than on free-standing posts. Do this by fixing a sturdy timber, 100 or 150 x 50mm (4 or 6 x 2in) in section and the length of the pergola, to the house wall using strong masonry fixings. This timber support is called a wall plate. The joists are fixed directly to the wall plate with joist hangers, or they can rest on top of the wall plate and be secured to it with diagonal screws or L-shaped brackets. The joists can, alternatively, be fixed to the wall at a sloping angle, rather like an unglazed lean-to greenhouse.

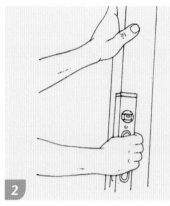

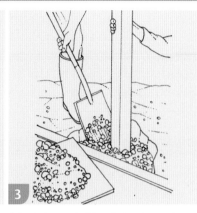

Mark out the outline of the pergola on the ground with pegs and string. Be sure to get the post locations right, and check that everything is square. Then dig the post holes, 60cm (24in) deep and about 30cm (12in) across. If your ground tends to be wet, dig the post holes a little deeper and spread a layer of hard core or scalpings in the bottom, compacting it well with a sturdy piece of timber.

Set a post upright in the first hole and hold it in place by packing a few half-bricks and stones into the hole. Check with a spirit level that it is exactly perpendicular, and that it is in the right place and the correct height above the ground. (It's easy to rush this, but a little extra time and trouble spent getting it spot-on at this stage will pay dividends later.) Repeat with the other posts.

Ask a helper to hold each post in turn in position while you fill the holes almost to the top with fairly stodgy concrete (mixed using 6:1 ballast : cement). You can slope the concrete down to help shed water away from the post. Leave a gap of about 50mm (2in) at the top so you can cover the concrete with soil when the structure is complete.

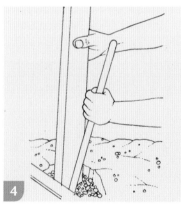

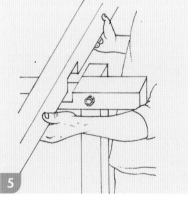

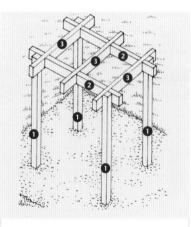

Check once more that the posts are still perpendicular and their tops level, then firm the concrete around each one with a piece of timber. Leave the concrete to harden for a few days before fixing the roof structure. That gives you plenty of time to cut evenly spaced, rectangular notches in the tops of the side beams, into which the joists will fit (*see* step 5). Position the end notches right next to the posts. You can cut the ends of the beams and joists neatly and evenly to whatever shape you fancy.

Once you have cut the notches in the side beams, use galvanized coach bolts to fix the beams lengthwise to the tops of the posts. Next, hold each joist in position so that there is an equal overhang on each side of the pergola and mark a notch in the bottom of the joist at each side, to correspond with the notches in the beams. Cut the notches, then fit the joists over the beams and secure them tightly from below with galvanized screws.

The completed pergola, showing how the posts (1), the two side beams (2) and the joists (3) are joined together.

### Don't forget

After you have cut pressure-treated timber, paint all the cut surfaces with timber preservative to prevent rot.

# Hands on: Gravel and chippings

For many purposes, a properly laid porous surface such as shingle, stone chippings or chipped bark can be an easier – and cheaper and more flexible – option than paving, concrete or tarmac. You don't have to worry as much about gradients, drainage, freezing or flooding, and it creates a more relaxed look than formal paving. Use single slabs as stepping stones set into the aggregate in areas that get regular trampling.

The timber edging here encloses a base layer of scalpings topped with Cotswold-style limestone chippings.

## Chipped bark

Don't dismiss chipped bark as a surfacing material, especially as a temporary solution. It's cheap, a doddle to lay, and it will ultimately improve the soil. If you decide to change the path, bark is easy to move, or it can be used as a mulch on beds and borders, or simply composted if you no longer want it. Of course, it's the surface of choice for play areas because it offers a relatively soft landing, but you can also use it for paths in the vegetable garden, informal paths elsewhere and for open areas around an arbour, gazebo or shed. Strips of timber, stones, tiles or bricks can be used to define the edges, and for a firmer, all-weather surface you can lay loose paving slabs on top of the bark as stepping-stones, making sure they are firmly bedded down.

## HOW TO lay a shingle path

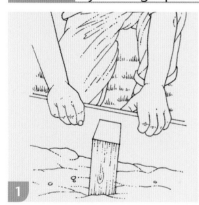

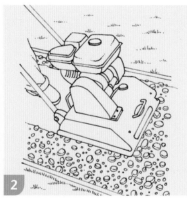

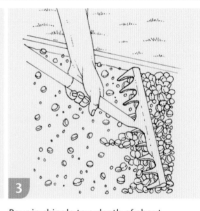

**1** Use string and pegs, or a trail of sand, to mark the edges of the path, then dig out the soil until you have a flat-bottomed trench about 10cm (4in) deep. Use pressure-treated softwood planking, 100mm x 25mm (4 x 1in), for the edging. Position it along the sides of the trench, and hammer in wooden pegs, 300mm (12in) long and 50 x 50mm (2 x 2in) in section, to hold it in position. The top of the pegs should be about 25mm (1in) below the top of the boards. Screw the boards to the pegs with galvanized screws.

**2** Spread scalpings about 75mm (3in) deep right across the trench and rake them level. Using a powered compactor plate (if you are laying the path yourself you can hire one) firm them into an even layer with no humps or hollows, finishing about 30mm (1¼in) below the top of the boards. This will give the path a good solid base, and compacting the scalpings down firmly will help prevent weeds coming through.

**3** Pour in shingle to a depth of about 25mm (1in) and rake until the surface is smooth and level. The boards that mark the edges should be slightly proud of the path's surface to prevent the gravel from spilling out over the adjoining area. The gravel may settle a little over time so keep it topped up. Regular raking works wonders and will keep your path looking smart, especially in autumn when the leaves are falling fast.

# Hands on: Wall fixings

Permanent wall supports for plants don't take long to fit, and a purpose-made structure makes tying in so much easier. Taut horizontal wires spaced about 45cm (18in) apart are fine for climbing roses, fan-trained fruit trees and wall shrubs with stiff stems, while trellis will give better support to the tendrils and soft shoots of fast-growing plants such as sweet peas and clematis.

## HOW TO put up wall wires

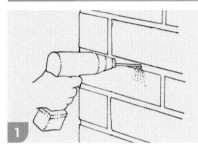

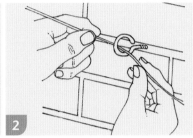

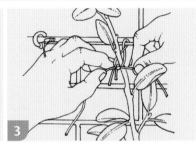

**1** Mark where you want to fix each wire in the mortar between bricks, with a soft pencil, checking that the line between them will be level with the brick courses. Drill a hole at either end for the vine eyes, and for long spans make additional holes at 1m (40in) intervals. Use wall plugs slightly longer than the screw thread of the vine eye, and drill holes just wide and deep enough to take the plugs.

**2** Push a wall plug into each hole and screw in a vine eye, finishing with the 'eye' facing sideways to keep the wire horizontal. Using strong galvanized wire, fix one end to your first vine eye by bending it round the eye to make a loop, then twisting the end round the wire to secure it. Run the wire through any intervening eyes, then stretch it taut and secure it to the eye at the other end.

**3** Tie the plants (not too tightly) to the wires at intervals. Use soft, strong ties or twine in a neutral colour. For plants that throw out new stems every year, ordinary jute twine is fine (and biodegradable). For plants with a more permanent framework, tie loosely with stronger twine or plant ties. Some plant ties can be reused, which is handy because you can easily reposition them as plants grow.

## HOW TO fix trellis to walls

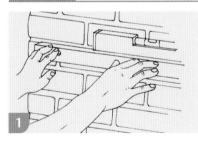

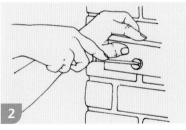

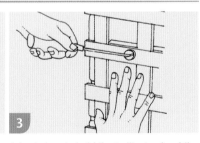

**1** Cut battens (50 x 25mm/2 x 1in in section) to the width of the trellis panel and paint them with preservative and/or exterior timber paint. Drill holes near each end, with additional ones evenly spaced between them if the panels are more than 1m (40in) wide. Mark the positions of the battens on the wall, about 30cm (12in) from the top and bottom of the trellis. Drill holes in the wall as for step 1 above, corresponding to the holes in the battens.

**2** Fix the battens to the wall with wall plugs and galvanized or brass screws long enough to make a secure fixing into the wall. Mark screw holes in the trellis to correspond with the battens behind, making sure that everything is level, and that the two sets of screws won't coincide. Hold the trellis in position against the wall to check everything is in the right place, then drill holes in the trellis just big enough to take the screws.

**3** Ask a helper to hold the trellis steady while you fix the first two screws, then screw in all the others. Dig a roomy hole for your climber or wall shrub, slightly away from the dry base of the wall, and put plenty of compost in the base. Put the plant in, fill in the hole, firm the soil and water in well to settle the roots. Finally, spread the plant's stems out along the base of the trellis, to ensure good coverage, and tie them in fairly loosely.

# Hands on: Lawns

A soft, green lawn is the ideal surface for relaxation, as well as for setting off your plants to perfection. Yet with today's trend towards smaller, lower-maintenance gardens, some consider lawns too much trouble. But if you have the space, and don't mind mowing, a lawn is as indispensable now as it ever was.

Turf is normally delivered in rolls like this. Don't leave it rolled up for long, though – it needs laying immediately.

Our temperate climate lends itself well to lawns. They are a brilliant foil for planting, and in a family garden there is no substitute for a lawn as a soft, spacious surface for children to play on. Don't think of it as an easy option, though – especially in difficult areas such as dry shade or where the soil regularly becomes waterlogged. A good lawn needs patience and care, and the edges must be kept trimmed. An edging of stones or bricks helps keep the perimeter neat; set them slightly lower than the grass so the mower can pass over the edge. Where a lawn and a border meet, a broad paved edging to the grass is ideal so that plants at the front of the border can spread forward, breaking up the edge without shading out the grass or making it difficult to mow.

## Mini meadows

Most gardens are too small for a full-scale meadow and they can be tricky to establish, but consider leaving a small patch of grass to grow longer, and allow wild flowers such as cowslips, daisies, speedwell, trefoil and clover to grow and seed themelves around. You'll be surprised how pretty these look, once you see them as flowers not weeds. The mini meadow will look beautiful in spring and early summer, and will be hugely beneficial to wildlife, especially insects. Mow neat paths through the longer grass, to save crushing it when you walk through and to make it clear that it's meant to be like that – you haven't just forgotten to mow!

A well-groomed, neatly edged lawn takes some looking after, even once it is well established, but in gardens where there is space its smooth green expanse is hard to beat as a foil for the plants that surround it.

## HOW TO lay turf

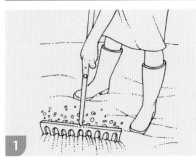  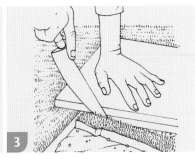

Prepare the ground thoroughly by forking or digging, removing large clods, stones and roots as you go. Then, taking your time, rake and tread the soil, still removing stones and lumps, and working in different directions to achieve a firm, level surface. Sprinkle a general fertilizer at the recommended rate and then rake once more so you finish with a covering of fine, level soil with no footprints.

Beginning with a straight edge, unroll and position the first turf, then the second, fitted closely up against the first, and so on – until you have a line of turves. Tamp the whole row down gently but firmly with the head of a rake to settle it into the soil. Lay a plank along the first row of turves to work from when laying the second row; don't walk on the freshly laid turf or the surface will become uneven. Make sure each turf is laid snugly against its neighbour and stagger the joints in each row. Repeat this process until the whole area is covered.

Still working from your plank, use an old, sharp kitchen knife to trim the edges of the new lawn to the shape you want. Water gently but thoroughly to help the turf bind, and keep watering every few days, preferably in the evening, unless it rains. If the turves dry out before they have rooted they will shrink and pull away from each other, leaving unsightly gaps. The turf should be rooted and growing within a couple of weeks, by which time the ground should have settled enough for you to mow for the first time, keeping the mower blades set high.

## HOW TO sow grass seed for a new lawn

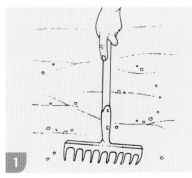  

The preparation is exactly as for laying turf (see above), but the timing is more critical. Early to mid-autumn is best, but mid- to late spring can also be a good time if it isn't too dry. You could use what is called the 'stale seedbed' technique. This means leaving the prepared ground for a couple of weeks to settle, and letting surface weed seeds germinate. You then hoe them off and give a final, light treading and raking.

If you want to sow seed by hand, use about 25–50g (1–2oz) per square metre (square yard). To achieve even coverage, divide the seed into two lots. Sprinkle one half, thinly, in one direction (say east to west) and the other half roughly at right angles to the first (north to south). Check the area once more and if there are any bare patches, sow extra seed to cover.

You won't be able to cover all the seed, but rake very lightly to work at least some of it into the soil. Leave no footprints! If necessary, lay twiggy prunings or tautly stretched netting over the newly sown lawn to keep off birds. The seed should germinate within a couple of weeks if you keep it well watered. Mow for the first time when the grass reaches about 5cm (2in), choosing a dry day and making sure your mower blades are sharp.

# Hands on: Water features

There's nothing quite like water for bringing a garden to life. The tradition of using water in gardens goes back to the earliest times and has been an integral part of almost every culture that has created gardens. The sight and sound of water are calming, relaxing and cooling, and a pond or water feature makes a wonderful focal point in any garden.

## When and where?

The best time for making a pond or water feature is late winter, when you won't have to rush, and there will be time for the water and surrounds to settle before you do your planting, ideally in mid-spring. Choose a dry spell for the digging if you can – it's less messy that way. Avoid frosty weather if you are using concrete or mortar.

Think about the best location for your water feature, and decide on its shape and form, during the previous growing season – so you can visualize the effect while the garden is in full swing. The site for a static pond should be reasonably level and sunny and, if your garden is on a slope, it should be at the bottom rather than the top. Avoid overhanging trees – you'd be surprised how quickly a small water feature or pond can fill up with leaves in autumn. It's nice to have room to stroll all the way round it, and convenient for maintenance too, so don't position it too close

Planting is the key to making a pond look natural. Just as in a border, try to choose an assortment of plant shapes to give visual interest.

to a boundary. A pleasant, sunny spot for a seat should be factored in as well. In winter, especially, it's lovely to be able to do your pond-watching from the house, so if possible locate it within easy viewing distance and keep the sight lines clear. Lastly, a wildlife pond, in particular, will benefit from being topped up with rainwater, so you could plan for an underground hose leading to the pond from a nearby water butt, fitted with a tap.

## 'Natural' ponds

Creating a 'natural' pond is the easiest way to make a real difference to your garden. It requires a certain amount of hard labour, but minimal construction expertise. Carefully chosen plants will, when settled in, do the work of a pump and filter, though you must be prepared for a certain amount of maintenance a few times a year, to keep the balance of planting right. With a bit of forethought and patience, it's easy to make the pond look natural. In many gardens this will be the best overall solution, for you and for wildlife. (*See* pages 74–5.)

## Formal pools

Building a formal pool is a task for a dedicated and proficient DIY enthusiast or a professional.

The job involves constructing a waterproof 'box' – usually rectangular or round – with vertical sides built from blockwork. The pond can be raised or part-raised, or completely sunk into the ground. It will need a pump and a filter, and therefore an electricity supply.

## Fountains or bubble-jet features

Water features of this kind are the safest and best option if you have young children, and they are relatively easy to construct. They're even available in kit form. The feature consists of a concealed, pre-formed underground reservoir that is covered with a reproduction millstone or other big stone, or an arrangement of large pebbles, from which a gentle water-jet emerges. The water is recycled into the reservoir. A solar-powered fountain even allows you to do without electricity, as long as you're happy to have running water only intermittently – when it's sunny.

## Streams

An artificial stream that doesn't look artificial is one of the more difficult water projects to pull off successfully, but if you have the right setting, and if you're up for something challenging, why not have a go? A feature like this really needs to be built into a natural slope to look right, and you have to be meticulous about covering every bit of the liner and concealing the pump and filter properly, for the illusion to really work. Consult a specialist water gardening book or website, or visit a dedicated water

A formal canal like this one in the Dillon Garden in Dublin is a job for a top-flight professional, but it's a fine example of how inspired design and classic materials can complement water – all set off by perfect planting.

gardening specialist. A good place to go for advice is the retail or online supplier of the pump, liner and other equipment; they may offer help or recommendations.

## Rills

This is the formal equivalent of a stream – a narrow, lined, waterproof channel, often with little waterfalls and perhaps a fountain at the end. Rills are found in some of the classic formal gardens. A rill is ambitious to plan and build, but it can look fantastic in an appropriate setting. As with a stream, the workings must be well hidden to avoid spoiling the elegant, streamlined appearance.

## Container ponds

If you have very little space you can make a water garden in a waterproofed half-barrel, trough or other container, either free-standing or sunk into the ground. Make it as large as you can – small bodies of water are much more susceptible to extremes of temperature.

Even a tiny garden can have a water feature in a container such as a large stone or ceramic pot or a wooden half-barrel. Choose a container to suit your garden. You can have either open water or a bubble-jet, like this.

make a 'natural' pond

## What you need
- Hosepipe, or string and canes
- Dry sand for marking out
- Mini-digger (for large ponds)
- Skip or trailer (if removing any or all of the spoil from the site)
- Spade and shovel
- Wheelbarrow
- Plank long enough to span the pond
- Long spirit level

## Materials
- Soft sand

This is used to smooth the surface of the hole.

- Pond underlay

This special polyester material (sold by stockists of pond liner) is laid underneath the liner to protect it. It is quite inexpensive, but before it became available thick layers of newspaper or old carpets were used instead.

- Pond liner

The heavy-duty, black rubber sheeting called butyl is best and will last longest. It is expensive, but so is having to do the whole thing again because the bargain-basement polythene liner you used sprang a leak. To make certain the liner is big enough, calculate how much you will need by measuring the maximum width and length of the pond, including the margin around the edge, then adding twice the maximum depth to each of these dimensions to give you the width and length of liner required.

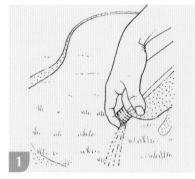

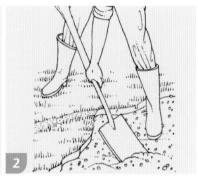

**1** Mark out the shape you want the pond to be, using first a hosepipe or a length of string held in place with canes. Next, mark out the perimeter by pouring dry sand gently out of a plastic bottle. Plan where to put the deepest area, which should be at least 60cm (24in) deep, and where to have gently sloping, beach-like edges and level underwater shelves (about 20cm/8in deep and 15cm/6in wide) to stand plants on. Earth slopes should be no steeper than 20 degrees from vertical, or the sides may collapse.

**2** Get digging! For large ponds, hiring a mini-digger may be worth the trouble and expense, but if you're reasonably fit, and take your time, there's no reason not to do the job by hand. It's cheaper and less disruptive. Keep some of the turf, which you may want to use for edging the pond. Put the spoil on a large tarpaulin beside the hole, keeping topsoil and subsoil separate if you plan to use the topsoil elsewhere in the garden. Remove as many stones as you can and try to make the bottom of the pond firm and flat.

## Don't forget

For smaller ponds, you might choose to use a pre-formed, rigid fibreglass shell. If you do, it's critical to make every part of the hole fit the shell exactly in order to support it evenly, with no air gaps or areas of loose soil beneath.

A contemporary natural pond, with a shaped deck providing a comfortable place to relax and watch the comings and goings of pondlife and birds. The cobbled 'beach' is ideal for letting birds and frogs reach shallow water, while the shrubs beyond the pond will provide essential cover.

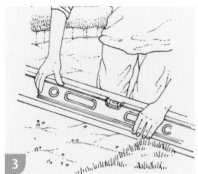

**3**

It's vital to ensure that the rim of the pond is level. Move soil around, either by building the edges up or bringing the level down until the edge looks the same height all the way round. Check that everything is level by laying a plank across the top of the hole, with a spirit level placed along it. For large ponds, mark the required level on pegs driven into the pond edges and run string across from one to another, again using a spirit level to check every so often that it's all horizontal.

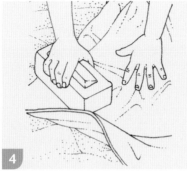

**4**

Spread an even layer of soft sand, at least 250mm (1in) thick, over the entire area. This makes a stone-free 'cushion' for the liner. Then cover the sand with special pond underlay and peg the edges in place. Recruit a helper for unfolding and laying the liner – it will be heavy and awkward to handle, and the less you have to move it about the less likely it is to get damaged. Unfold the liner centrally across the pond, then adjust the edges. Don't walk on it. Hold the edges in place temporarily with bricks, smooth boulders or short planks.

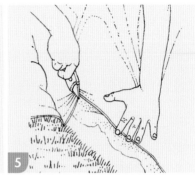

**5**

The exciting bit! Turn on the hose to fill the pond. Adjust the liner as necessary during this process so that it hugs the shape of the hole, and make sure any folds are small, tidy ones. Let the whole thing settle overnight, then cut off the edges of the liner to leave a 30cm (12in) margin beyond the water's edge.

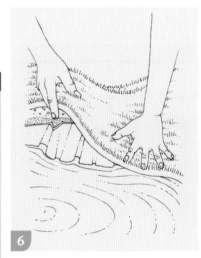

**6**

## Pond safety

■ Young children and ponds are a worrying combination, and you may decide to avoid open water until your children are older. A toddler can drown in only a tiny amount of water. One option, however, is to cover the pond with a decorative rigid metal grille.

■ Before deciding where to put the pond, check whether there are any underground services such as electricity or telephone cables, drains, or gas, oil or water pipes in the vicinity. You will be digging deep, and you don't want any nasty surprises when the hole is half dug.

■ Site the pond well away from trees with toxic leaves or seeds, such as laburnum, laurel or yew, to avoid contaminating the water.

■ Don't use garden chemicals or treated timber near a pond.

■ Avoid using slippery materials near the pond edge.

■ Always use a qualified electrician to wire up any pumps, filters and lighting that are connected to the mains supply.

Cover the exposed edges of the liner. This is important both to make the pond look natural and to prevent the liner from perishing in the sun. Use turf, which can run down into the water, or paving stones, which should overhang the edge slightly. Decking (either as a terrace or a boardwalk) also works well beside water. Let things settle before you introduce plants. Be prepared for the water to take time to clear: an initial period of murkiness is quite normal.

## Plants for water

Whatever type of water feature you choose, it is likely to have some kind of planting in and around it. Plants are essential to keep the water sweet in ponds without pumps and filters. They also provide a vital habitat for many kinds of water creature, from snails – these do a great algae-hoovering job that helps keep the water clean – to dragonflies. These beautiful creatures depend on plants: first as a place to lay their eggs and then, when the next generation matures, as a means of emerging from the water. Choose as many native plants as possible: they are kinder to the environment and to wildlife, and many of them are as beautiful as their exotic cousins.

### Underwater plants

Submerged plants such as pondweeds play a vital housekeeping role in aquatic ecosystems by giving off oxygen directly into the water and by helping to control the spread of algae. Some of the common oxygenators, such as the Canadian pondweed *Elodea canadensis*, are too thuggish for garden ponds, and it is better to use the native pondweeds that are available in good garden centres. These include native species of milfoil such as *Myriophyllum spicatum* and *M. verticillatum*, and *Potamogeton crispus* (curled pondweed).

### Deep-water plants

Some of the most frequently seen aquatic plants need deepish water for their roots but carry their leaves and flowers on the surface. They are usually planted in perforated plastic baskets to keep them in place. Baskets with fine plastic mesh, which don't need lining, are a good choice.

Everyone is familiar with the round leaves and gorgeous, waxy flowers of waterlilies, but that doesn't mean they are easy to grow. They don't like moving water, or even a fountain, and they won't flower without plenty of sunlight. Above all, you need to choose the right water lily for the size and depth of your pond. Many white ones are too vigorous for small ponds. *Nymphaea tetragona* is a good miniature white, happy in only 25cm (10in) of water in even the tiniest pond. The fragrant *N.* 'Walter Pagels' is larger, but still quite compact, with creamy-white double flowers. Pink and red ones to look

Waterlilies are a must for many pond owners, but there are so many to choose from. *Nymphaea* 'Rose Arey' ticks most of the necessary boxes: it's early-flowering, fragrant, not too vigorous – and rather beautiful.

out for include *N.* 'Rose Arey' and *N.* 'Froebelii'. A small to medium-sized formal pool makes a perfect setting for them and, if they are happy, they will flower for months.

The hardier arum lilies, for example *Zantedeschia aethiopica* 'Crowborough', will usually survive outdoors all winter if their crowns are in deepish water. Elegant, shapely white flower spathes make this a plant of distinction, especially beautiful at dusk.

## Marginal plants

These are the plants that grow on the shelf at the edge of a pond, with just their roots and lower stems submerged. They too can be planted in perforated plastic baskets. *Butomus umbellatus* (flowering rush) is a beautiful wild water plant, with pale pink flowers, not unlike those of an allium, in high summer. *Caltha palustris* (kingcup or marsh marigold) has bright golden flowers ('water-blobs') in early spring, which have always made it a firm favourite. The sword-like leaves of irises emerging from the water in spring suit both wild and more formal ponds; *Iris laevigata* (Japanese water iris) has many cultivated forms with flowers in different colours, as well as one with silver-white variegated leaves. The species is a beautiful lavender blue. *Menyanthes trifoliata* (bog bean) is a rather exotic-looking native with leaves like a broad bean. If it likes your pond it will produce spikes of beautiful, frilly pale-pink flowers in spring. And nothing smells as refreshing on a hot day as *Mentha aquatica* (water mint); its flowers are pretty too.

Many native water plants are easily as attractive as their exotic alien counterparts. Marsh marigold or kingcup (above, top) and bogbean (above) are two to try for starters, and there are lots more.

## Waterside wild flowers

The area around a pond lends itself to a special kind of planting, linking the water with the rest of the garden and perhaps taking advantage of boggy ground (*see also* pages 136–7). Wild flowers add welcome colour and interest to the damp grass around a natural pond, and are a magnet for bees and butterflies. Here are some to try:

*Angelica sylvestris* (wild angelica)
*Cardamine pratensis* (lady's smock)
*Filipendula ulmaria* (meadowsweet)
*Fritillaria meleagris* (snakeshead fritillary)
*Geum rivale* (water avens)
*Lychnis flos-cuculi* (ragged robin)
*Parnassia palustris* (grass of Parnassus)
*Ranunculus acris* (meadow buttercup)
*Valeriana officinalis* (common valerian)
*Veronica beccabunga* (brooklime)

## Rejuvenating a pond

Ponds soon become clogged and overgrown if they are neglected for any length of time. Renovating a pond is a wet and messy job, but it is also very satisfying. You will need a lawn rake to pull out all the plants, piling them on the bank as you go. Take care when raking – if you are too enthusiastic about it, you could puncture the pond liner. Then clear out as much as possible of the accumulated gunge at the bottom of the pond. Re-plant healthy-looking pieces of the plants you want to keep, and treat yourself to a few new ones. Leave the rest of the plant pile overnight, so any trapped water creatures have a chance to escape, and next day tidy and weed the surrounds. Late winter and early spring are the best times for a clear out, but avoid disturbing frog and toad spawn.

## What not to plant

Certain non-native water plants have escaped from cultivation and in some places have formed damagingly vigorous colonies in natural watercourses, upsetting their delicate ecological balance, threatening native species and costing a lot to eradicate. Water plants you should never buy, even though you may see them on sale or recommended in old books, include:

*Azolla filiculoides* (fairy fern)
*Crassula helmsii* (Australian swamp stonecrop or New Zealand pygmy weed)
*Eichhornia crassipes* (water hyacinth)
*Hydrocotyle ranunculoides* (floating pennywort)
*Lagarosiphon major* (curly waterweed)
*Myriophyllum aquaticum* (parrot's feather or Brazilian water milfoil)
*Pistia stratiotes* (water lettuce)

There are other common plants that, despite some of them being native and attractive, are simply too large and vigorous for a small garden pond. These include:

*Gunnera manicata*
*Iris pseudacorus* (yellow flag)
*Lythrum salicaria* (purple loosestrife)
*Sparganium erectum* (branched bur-reed)
*Typha latifolia* (great reedmace or bulrush)

Gardens are getting smaller, and nowadays many homes in towns – especially new houses – have only a tiny outdoor space to call their own. This is ideal for busy people who have little time or enthusiasm for gardening, or for older people who may have downsized from a large garden. Yet even the smallest garden can work brilliantly well, provided it is thoughtfully planned and has a simple, cohesive design.

**'Less is more'**

This may be an overused phrase, but it really does apply when you're dealing with a very small garden. Visual tricks may make the space seem bigger, but in terms of how much you should actually fit in there's a definite limit. To look and feel right, any garden needs some open space, and if you cram in too many features you will end up with an overcrowded, cramped garden that is hard to maintain and no pleasure to be in – like a room with too much furniture. When allocating space to particular features, always remember to allow enough 'elbow room' – space to move about around a table and chairs, for example, and room to pass comfortably through doors and gates, even when you're carrying a basket full of wet laundry or a large sack of compost.

**Planting opportunities**

A small town garden surrounded by buildings may be shadier than you would wish (*see* pages 130–1), but it will also be sheltered. This gives you the opportunity to grow a range of foliage plants that would not stand up to the drying and damaging effects of wind in a more open site.

Try dramatic ferns such as tree ferns or *Matteuccia struthiopteris*, or the evergreen native fern *Polystichum setiferum*, with *Vinca minor* (lesser periwinkles) for spring and hostas for summer. Golden foliage is excellent for adding brightness to semi-shaded areas, though many golden plants will darken to green if the shade is very deep. Shapely white flowers such as *Zantedeschia aethiopica* (arum lilies), *Clematis* 'Marie Boisselot', *Dicentra spectabilis* 'Alba' or the white foxglove *Digitalis purpurea* f. *albiflora*, take on a starring role in shady places, while

Small but perfectly formed. This is a tiny area of a tiny garden, but it has everything a satisfying design needs – structure, focal points, variety and year-round interest.

foliage plants such as the white-variegated honesty, *Lunaria annua* var. *albiflora* 'Alba Variegata', or *Arum italicum* subsp. *italicum* 'Marmoratum' show off their intricate patterning much better in low light.

Vertical planting also comes into its own in a small garden. Climbers of all kinds, trained up obelisks or trellis screens, will emphasize the third dimension, height. Closer to the ground, it's a good idea to include spiky plants and slender, upright grasses such as *Calamagrostis* x *acutiflora* 'Overdam' or *Miscanthus sinensis* 'Morning Light' to lead the eye upwards from the limited ground space. Raised beds also make good use of the vertical space, and can be planted with treasures such as auriculas and other specialist plants that demand to be seen close-up.

### Hanging baskets and window boxes
A small garden is likely to have a close relationship with its house. Window boxes and hanging baskets connect the two even more closely and are an invaluable way of increasing limited

## Space-saving equipment

Manufacturers of all kinds of garden paraphernalia now cater better than ever for gardeners with limited space. If you shop around you will find ingenious space-saving versions of all those things you thought you didn't have room for, such as:

- Slimline water butt
- Lean-to mini-greenhouse
- Folding wheelbarrow
- Seat with tool storage box underneath
- Folding willow obelisk
- Folding tables and chairs

planting space. Use them for fragrant plants, which you can appreciate both indoors and out, or for a supply of culinary herbs within easy reach of the kitchen. Sunshine isn't essential, as long as you choose suitable plants. Indeed, containers in very sunny spots can dry out rapidly on hot days, but those sitting in the shade require much less attention.

In tight spaces, simple ideas generally work best. ① A highly original herb garden makes a unique feature of a shady passageway. ② The sunny wall of a cottage lends itself to conventional planting – well-maintained hanging baskets bursting with summer colour.

## All-year-round greenery for small spaces

■ *Fatsia japonica* This is the ultimate architectural evergreen, with great hand-shaped leaves that cast interesting shadows. Cut it back each spring if you want to keep it bushy, and don't let it get too dry.

■ *Ilex aquifolium* The many variegated cultivars of holly work equally well as shrubs or small trees. They are shade-tolerant, and can be kept to size by pruning once or twice a year.

■ *Laurus nobilis* Bay is a favourite for courtyards, entrances and other small spaces. It will look smart all year round if you keep it pruned to shape in summer. Prune it with secateurs, not shears, to avoid unsightly brown edges on leaves cut in half.

■ *Osmanthus* x *burkwoodii* This dark broadleaved evergreen has dense foliage, and fragrant white blossom in early spring.

■ *Pittosporum tenuifolium* With their attractive pale-green leaves and dark stems, pittosporums never become oppressive. There are cultivars with pretty purple or variegated foliage.

■ *Taxus baccata* Yew is one of the plants that are suitable for the fashionable Japanese technique of 'cloud pruning', which results in a tree with tightly clipped blobs of foliage (the clouds) linked by short stretches of bare trunk from which all shoots are removed. The effect is much lighter than that of solid, clipped yew.

# Planting by design

Putting together a planting scheme is a bit like painting a picture. You are using a palette of plants to create an apparently seamless (but in fact carefully contrived) blend of satisfying composition and effective colours. The composition angle is sometimes forgotten in garden planning, but it's an important component if you want your collection of plants to work together as a scheme that looks good all year. A border needs contrasts of shape, scale and texture, sequences to lead your eye, and focal points to act as punctuation marks. Without these, it can easily become a confusing, pointless jumble.

# Using plants

Everyone has their favourite plants, and we should all have the ones we like best in our gardens. But if a planting scheme is to succeed as a balanced, harmonious whole, it's also vital to recognize the role that each different plant will play as part of the team effort. But don't just make a collection of plants, with one of each kind, like specimens. Herbaceous plants, especially, make more impact when at least some of them are grouped in drifts or clumps of several individual plants.

Evergreens, bare branches and shapely seedheads emerge as summer foliage and colours fade, making a garden that is still full of visual interest in winter.

## Structure

To some plants, forming the bones of a planting scheme just comes naturally. Depending on the space you have to play with, these structural plants might be formal, clipped evergreens such as domes, cubes or cones of box or yew, positioned to accentuate a path or mark corners; they could include one or more distinctive trees used as stand-alone specimens; or perhaps a large architectural plant that is so striking it simply stands out from the crowd. Climbers trained up obelisks are another option.

Structural plants should be used with two main things in mind. First, they should contrast with the many less conspicuous 'filler' plants of the growing season, serving as a framework that helps to hold the scheme together. Secondly, they should also provide structure in the dormant season. It's well worth considering how plants will contribute in winter. A few carefully chosen, distinctive plants can make all the difference between a garden that has sunk into off-season tiredness, making you look the other way, and a picture that gives pleasure whenever you glimpse it.

## Grouping plants

Make structural plants your first priority when planning your border, whether on paper or on the ground. They are difficult to position correctly at a later stage, and there may well be reasons for putting them in particular places – hiding an eyesore perhaps, or aligning with something else to create a focal point. The next step is to combine them with complementary plants of different shapes, with the structural plants as the dominant feature. Take care to restrict the number of dominant plants. Adjacent planting should be a foil for these, and not steal their thunder. Group complementary plants in drifts, perhaps with an 'outlier' just beyond the end of the group for a more natural look.

Don't grade a border strictly in height, from back to front, like a team photo. Plants at the back must be visible when in flower, but a few tall grasses or alliums at the front will add depth and richness.

There are no universal rules for putting plants together, and you will develop your own techniques. A successful border will usually have been contrived – but it should always look effortless.

## Shape

One of the elements that makes the plant world so fascinating is the diversity of shapes within it. The variety is almost endless, but for the purposes of planning a planting scheme, plant shapes can be simplified into a handful of groups. Generally, a recipe for a successful border will include some from each.

## Vertical plants

With a small footprint in relation to their height, the best strongly vertical plants, in design terms, have distinct upright lines – tall, slender flower spikes, or sword-shaped leaves, or sometimes both. This group also includes some conifers and other shrubs and trees (*see* page 105). These emphatic plants, even those that are not very tall, can contribute valuable structure to a border.

## Horizontal plants

Plants with strong horizontal shapes range from those with sideways-spreading, rounded or spoon-shaped leaves to those with flat plates of flowers or daisy-like blooms. Also in this group are shrubs with a layered or tiered effect, or with a spreading branch structure. Ideal for border edges where there is room for them to extend laterally, they also contrast vividly with the 'verticals', and the two together form an excellent basis for many a planting scheme.

## Domed plants

Included in this group are compact evergreen shrubs such as dwarf hebes and santolina, and plants,

### Plants with strong shapes

**BOLD FOLIAGE**
*Cordyline australis*
*Cynara cardunculus*
*Fatsia japonica*
*Ficus carica*
*Hosta sieboldiana*
*Humulus lupulus* 'Aureus'
*Matteuccia struthiopteris*
*Rheum palmatum* 'Atrosanguineum'
*Ricinus communis*

**VERTICALS**

| Spiky leaves | Spiky flowers |
|---|---|
| *Cordyline* (below) | *Acanthus* |
| *Crocosmia* | *Delphinium* |
| *Iris* | *Digitalis* |
| *Kniphofia* | *Eremurus* (below) |
| *Libertia* | *Kniphofia* |
| *Phormium* (below) | *Lupinus* |
| *Sisyrinchium* | *Verbascum* |
| *Yucca* | *Veronicastrum* |

**HORIZONTALS**
**Foliage**
*Bergenia*
*Brunnera*
*Cotoneaster horizontalis*
*Cyclamen*
*Hosta*
*Rheum*
*Viburnum davidii*

**Flowers**
*Achillea*
*Euphorbia polychroma*
*Helenium*
*Rudbeckia*
*Sedum*
*Viburnum plicatum* f. *tomentosum* 'Mariesii'

usually herbaceous, that grow in bun-shaped clumps. These are useful on corners where a low 'full stop' is needed.

## Filler plants

Softening the lines of the more definite shapes, these plants fill gaps and help to knit a scheme together. They have a range of textures and habits from fluffy to creeping, and good examples are *Viola cornuta*, trailing campanulas and the 'wandering' perennial geraniums.

### Plants for texture

**LIGHT AND FLUFFY**
*Alchemilla mollis*
*Astilbe*
*Crambe cordifolia*
*Cryptomeria japonica* 'Elegans Compacta'
*Eupatorium maculatum* Atropurpureum Group
*Euphorbia cyparissias* 'Fens Ruby'
*Foeniculum vulgare* 'Purpureum'
*Gypsophila paniculata*
*Nigella damascena*
*Spiraea* 'Arguta'
*Stipa tenuissima*
*Thalictrum aquilegiifolium*

**BOLD AND LEATHERY**
x *Fatshedera lizei*
*Fatsia japonica*
*Rheum palmatum* 'Atrosanguineum' (below)
*Rodgersia podophylla*
*Viburnum davidii*

A dramatic foliage composition, seen at its best in late spring. From top: *Polygonatum* x *hybridum* (Solomon's seal), *Rodgersia podophylla*, *Iris pseudacorus* 'Variegata' and *Hosta* 'Halcyon'.

## Texture

A garden that will look good for many months of the year must draw from the whole spectrum of plant material, and that includes textures. In your beds and borders, plant groupings that exploit contrasting textures, as well as shapes and colours, will always have the edge, enabling you to get more 'plant power' out of even the smallest space. It's amazing to think of all the different textures that plants can contribute to a scheme – woolly, waxy, stiff, papery, silky, shiny, matt and many more (*see* page 110). And it's not just the flowers and leaves: seedheads, fruits, stems and bark all add to the effect.

## Colour

Any garden designer will tell you that to build a satisfying planting scheme you have to think about *all* the visual properties of a plant. But colour is the obvious one for most people, and the one they tend to feel most strongly about. Favourite colours are deeply ingrained. Colour is often a matter of 'gut reaction' or personal taste that is certain to influence your choice of plants, but in garden design try to expand your horizons and get to grips with the power of different colours to create particular effects.

## Combining colours

A lot of the skill in planning a border lies in the way you combine colours. A good means of learning how to do this is to study planting schemes at flower shows and in gardens. Record, in notes and photographs, what works and why. This will also help you to manage the tricky business of getting flower colours to coincide: a colour combination is useless if the plants end up flowering at different times.

A colour wheel – a device used by artists and designers, setting out the colours of the spectrum in a circle (*see* right) – can be a helpful illustration of some of the ways in which colours work with each other. Colours that are directly opposite on the wheel make the best contrasts: lime green and purple, orange and deep blue, or red and green. Colour harmonies work best if they are chosen from colours that are adjacent to each other on the wheel: yellow, orange and red, for example.

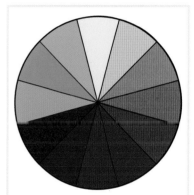

A simple colour wheel is a handy design tool showing the ways in which colours relate to each other. Colours that harmonize are adjacent to each other on the wheel, while colours that make good contrasts are opposite each other.

But remember that when planning a colour scheme you may not have a completely blank canvas. A strongly coloured existing tree or shrub such as a photinia or a forsythia, or even a high red-brick wall (*see* page 31), may need to be factored in, and will certainly limit your palette in that area of the garden.

## Using colours

The best plant combinations often come about completely by chance.

Trial and error with colours can be entertaining, and happy accidents, when plants combine themselves beautifully, do happen. But you have to wait for them, so it's a slow route to success. It definitely pays to have some clear ideas on colours and their effects at the back of your mind, well before you start to put plants together.

## Blue

Of all flower colours, blue is the hardest to capture in photographs. Perhaps it is this elusiveness that helps make it such a special, and popular, colour in the garden. Everyone loves blue. Cool, calming, sophisticated and versatile, it works as a great foil for so many other colours: with yellows and whites in those long-awaited, fresh schemes of early spring; with rich reds and violet to make a jewel-like picture with all the richness of a Persian carpet; or in startling, two-colour combinations to contrast tellingly with lime green or orange. Blue also shows up well in low light, especially at dawn and dusk when it seems to come to the fore.

## Purple

Sombre and rather dull on its own, purple goes brilliantly with silver and grey, and this is a good colour scheme for a dry, sunny site – perhaps a gravel garden – where you could use drought-resistant Mediterranean shrubs with tulips, irises and alliums. Purple or bronze foliage makes a rich, exciting backdrop to red flowers: the popular *Dahlia* 'Bishop of Llandaff' has just this combination. Purples and blues also make a striking but cooler contrast with lime green plants such as euphorbias or *Alchemilla mollis*.

## Pink

Use paler shades of pink with white, blue and lilac in a classic pastel scheme, or darker pinks in a glowing mix of rich, sultry hues with deep blues, reds and purples. Either of these combinations works well with silver, bronze or green foliage. Pink and yellow can clash unpleasantly – beware of forsythia and flowering

The garden at Great Dixter is famous for exciting and inventive colour combinations – here alliums, honesty and campanulas contrast with golden wallflowers, in the Solar garden.

A daring Dixter partnership: *Salvia involucrata* 'Bethellii' clashing loudly with *Dahlia* 'Chimborazo'.

### Orange

Orange is always an exciting colour, whether used in harmonious schemes with red and yellow, or in more daring contrasts with deep blue, purple or bronze. *Ajuga reptans*, with its blue flower spikes in spring, is a good partner for orange tulips, while orange geums, poppies or pot marigolds are good with spiky blue salvias a little later in the year.

### Yellow

Yellow seems to be the colour of spring in the garden – all that forsythia, all those daffodils. It can easily take over again in late summer, with sunflowers, rudbeckias and goldenrod. Some people aren't keen on yellow, and it can be difficult to use with other colours. But yellow does have a capacity to cheer things up that no other colour can rival, and it's worth thinking about how to use it cleverly. Along with white, it is great for brightening up dull places. Use golden-variegated shrubs, for instance, to bring the illusion of sunshine to a corner that doesn't get much of the real thing (*see* page 125). But be careful – many golden-leaved plants will only keep their bright colour if they receive a certain amount of light, reverting to green if it's too gloomy for them.

### Green

This is the most soothing and restorative of all colours. Where there is no greenery, the lack of it is deeply felt. An all-green garden (daring, in a way), can be very effective, especially in shade, transforming a small town garden, perhaps, into a cool, tranquil retreat. A green scheme, however, needs

currant or cherry doing one another no favours in spring if planted too closely. But pale creamy yellow with a dark pink, such as a magenta cranesbill, can work very well.

### Red

'Hot' borders with a red theme are eye-catching to say the least, and can be a great way to enjoy a fling of rip-roaring bold colour, especially in late summer and autumn. Purple, silver and green foliage all work well as an accompaniment, and there is a surprising number of wonderful red flowers to choose from: roses, clematis, dahlias, daylilies, penstemons and many berrying shrubs. The National Trust gardens at Hidcote, in Gloucestershire, and Tintinhull, in Somerset, both have glorious red borders. Plan a visit, or look at photographs, for inspiration.

Green need never be dull. Beth Chatto's planting of shuttlecock fern (*Matteuccia struthiopteris*) with *Rodgersia podophylla* has all the textural contrast you could wish for.

careful handling because the interest will depend on plant shapes and textures, and without enough variety it could easily be dull. Ferns, hostas and shade-tolerant grasses are a good combination for a calming scheme – but admittedly it may not be to everyone's taste.

Green is a great mediator when it comes to warring colours. A meadow can contain every colour but never looks garish because of the tempering effect of the grass, and plenty of foliage in a border prevents an exciting mix turning into a messy riot of clashing colours.

## White and silver

White flowers and silver, or grey, foliage (*see* pages 91, 115) really come into their own at dusk, standing out in the gloaming when other colours can no longer be distinguished (*see* page 114). Choose plants with interesting shapes to exploit this – the steely, sharp outlines of eryngiums, the fans of variegated irises or the delicate froth of gypsophila. Distinctively shaped white plants set against a dark background, such as a yew hedge, will really stand out. A dark or shady backdrop is also ideal for the great trumpets of *Lilium regale*. Like many other white flowers, these have a swooning fragrance on summer evenings. White is a component of all the pastel colours and combines well with them. It's also a lovely fresh colour to use in spring with blues, greens and yellows.

## Variegated plants

It may often seem, especially if you go to a specialist plant sale, as if every single plant has at least one variegated form – that is, one with leaves that have cream or yellow markings. From a design angle, variegated plants can be hugely useful as accent features, or to brighten dull corners. But there's no getting away from the fact that variegated plants tend to draw attention to themselves. If you overdo it you will end up with too many plants clamouring for the limelight.

Most variegated plants grow more slowly than their green-leaved counterparts, because they contain less of the green pigment chlorophyll, which enables photosynthesis – the process by which plants turn sunlight into energy for growth. Certain variegated plants are clearly suitable for small spaces but some are such weaklings that they are best avoided or you will spend your life coaxing them to cling on to theirs.

That said, there are many very good variegated plants: see a selection below.

**VARIEGATED GROUND COVER FOR SHADE**
*Arum italicum* subsp. *italicum* 'Marmoratum'
*Cyclamen hederifolium*
*Hedera canariensis* 'Gloire de Marengo'
*Hedera colchica* 'Sulphur Heart'
*Hedera helix* 'Oro di Bogliasco'
*Hosta* 'Wide Brim'
*Lamium maculatum* 'White Nancy'
*Pulmonaria saccharata*

**VARIEGATED SPIKY PLANTS**
*Iris pallida* 'Variegata'
*Iris pseudacorus* 'Variegata'
*Phormium cookianum* subsp. *hookeri* 'Cream Delight'
*Sisyrinchium striatum* 'Aunt May'
*Yucca filamentosa* 'Bright Edge'

**VARIEGATED HERBACEOUS PLANTS**
*Astrantia major* 'Sunningdale Variegated'
*Brunnera macrophylla* 'Hadspen Cream'
*Euphorbia characias* 'Silver Swan'
*Mentha suaveolens* 'Variegata'
*Sedum erythrostictum* 'Frosty Morn'

**VARIEGATED GRASSES**
*Calamagrostis* x *acutiflora* 'Overdam'
*Carex morrowii* 'Fisher's Form'
*Miscanthus sinensis* 'Morning Light'
*Miscanthus sinensis* 'Zebrinus'

**VARIEGATED TREES AND SHRUBS**
*Acer platanoides* 'Drummondii'
*Cornus alba* 'Elegantissima'
*Cornus controversa* 'Variegata'
*Sambucus nigra* 'Marginata'
*Weigela* 'Florida Variegata'

**VARIEGATED EVERGREENS**
*Euonymus fortunei* 'Silver Queen'
*Ilex aquifolium* 'Handsworth New Silver'
*Luma apiculata* 'Glanleam Gold'
*Osmanthus heterophyllus* 'Goshiki'
*Rhamnus alaternus* 'Argenteovariegata'
*Viburnum tinus* 'Variegatum'

White foxgloves and lupins standing out among a sea of foliage – an especially effective planting at dusk.

The design elements of a garden, like those of an interior, work in subtle ways to create a mood that you pick up on as soon as you step into the space. Colour, light, scent, sound, stillness, temperature and humidity are among the factors that make up this complex and powerful cocktail.

## Light and shade

Light and shade, and the contrast between them, are key considerations in setting the mood of a particular space. Subdued light conditions promote feelings of calm, and of welcome coolness even during hot weather. Bright light can be invigorating in spring, oppressive and overwhelming in summer, relaxing and perhaps a touch wistful in autumn. You might use light and shade to create a sense of mystery, where a sunlit path disappears into dappled tree cover perhaps, or of anticipation, where a tempting patch of sunlight is seen beyond an area of shade.

## Colour and mood

Use plant colour to influence the mood of a garden and experiment with some of these well-established links to see if they work for you:

| | |
|---|---|
| Calming | white, blue |
| Cooling | blue, green, white |
| Cheerful | yellow, orange |
| Mysterious | purple, 'black' |
| Romantic | pink, white, lilac |
| Exciting | red, orange |

## Movement and sound

Gentle movement and the sound it often produces can have a soothing and relaxing effect. You can bring movement into a garden by using water – maybe just a simple bubble-jet, wall spout or solar-powered fountain. And easier still, introduce some plants that move with the slightest breath of wind, for instance a birch tree or one of the grasses, for example the shimmering, silky *Stipa tenuissima*. (*See also* pages 110–11.)

## Scent

There's no doubt that scents have a powerful effect on mood and emotions, working in complex and subtle ways to evoke memories and feelings. The whole thing is very subjective – so the best advice is just to choose those that you like best. (*See also* pages 110–11.)

Contrasting moods: ① vibrant and stimulating, with *Crocosmia* 'Lucifer' leading the cast in a late-summer border; ② cool and calming with a classic pairing of water and willow.

## Moody plants

**CALMING BLUES**
*Anchusa azurea* 'Loddon Royalist'
*Caryopteris* x *clandonensis* 'Heavenly Blue'
*Ceanothus* 'Concha'
*Ceratostigma willmottianum*
*Delphinium*
*Eryngium alpinum*
*Geranium* 'Rozanne'
*Hibiscus syriacus* 'Bluebird'
*Iris sibirica* 'Tropic Night'
*Nigella damascena*

**EXCITING REDS**
*Crocosmia* 'Lucifer'
*Dahlia* 'Bishop of Llandaff'
*Papaver orientale* Goliath Group 'Beauty of Livermere'
*Persicaria amplexicaule* 'Firetail'
*Pyracantha* 'Saphyr Rouge'
*Rosa* 'Geranium'
*Tulipa* 'Couleur Cardinal'
*Viburnum opulus* 'Compactum'

**CHEERFUL YELLOWS**
*Achillea filipendulina* 'Gold Plate'
*Anthemis tinctoria* 'E.C. Buxton'
*Hemerocallis* 'Corky'
*Kniphofia* 'Bees' Lemon'
*Mahonia* x *media* 'Winter Sun'
*Meconopsis cambrica*
*Narcissus* 'Tête-à-Tête'
*Rosa* 'Graham Thomas'

# Trees

Planting a tree is often the easiest, most economical and most successful way to create height in a garden. Of course, it requires a little patience, but a suitable tree, thoughtfully positioned, can be invaluable, providing not only a strong focal point, but also screening, shelter, shade, perhaps flowers and fruit to enjoy, and cover for wildlife. The right tree can be important in achieving a particular design effect – for example an acer in a Japanese garden – but remember it will only be the right tree if it also suits its growing conditions.

Winter tree shapes are endlessly intriguing. This unusual but short-lived tracery, caught in perfect light conditions, belongs to *Robinia pseudoacacia* 'Lace Lady', clinging on to its leaves after an early frost.

## Choosing a tree

Garden trees are a big investment, not so much in terms of cash (true, they aren't cheap – though a good tree will be worth every penny) but because they will occupy precious garden space for a long time to come. Choosing the right tree is therefore a major decision. The tree needs to be happy in the conditions you can offer it, and you must be happy to live with and look at that particular tree 365 days a year.

So, before you rush home from the garden centre with the prettiest tree you could find there this week, here are a few things to think about.

## Size and spread

If space is limited, it is much better (for you and for the tree) to select a variety that is naturally compact, rather than one that is going to involve you in constant saw-and-secateur battles, or regular bills from a tree surgeon, simply to keep it within its allotted place.

## Growing conditions

Some types of tree will naturally be more tolerant of dry, chalky soil; others won't mind a windy boundary; and a problematic damp spot in your garden will be meat and drink to some species. Finding out which trees are likely to enjoy life with you is not only easy, but also well worth the effort. A tree that is struggling with its growing conditions will never be an asset, no matter how well it might suit the style of your garden.

## Seasons of interest

For those of us with limited space, a tree that works hard to contribute to

### Right tree, wrong place

Avoid planting certain trees in particular places. For example, you may live to regret putting a thorny tree too close to where you walk or sit. And *Morus nigra* (black mulberry) will stain paving (and clothes, and children!) with its luscious but messy dark fruits. Some trees, such as some of the limes, attract aphids that exude a sticky honeydew, which you will soon know all about if you have to park your car under them.

the garden scene during two or three seasons of the year will be a better investment than a tree that has gorgeous blossom for one week and looks dull as ditchwater for the other 51. So find out if it has attractive foliage, colourful berries,

good autumn tints or interesting bark in the winter months.

## Living with trees

Some trees (most notoriously willows and poplars) have questing roots that must not be allowed anywhere near buildings or drains. Many other fast-growing woodland trees, such as sycamore and beech, are almost as unsuitable for the average garden. Even some popular garden trees are less than ideal. *Robinia*, for example, has brittle branches that can snap off unannounced. Insurance companies tend to disapprove of trees planted near buildings, especially if they are of an unsuitable type. But as a general rule, most ornamental garden trees are likely to be fine, as long you plant them at least as far away from buildings as their expected mature height.

The Judas tree (*Cercis siliquastrum*) makes a fine feature for a sunny spot.

The dazzling white bark of *Betula utilis* var. *jacquemontii* – a favourite tree for contemporary gardens.

## Trees for a light canopy

People are often wary of planting a tree because of the shade it will cast, and this is something worth thinking about when choosing. If you go for a tree with a spreading canopy and dense foliage, it will have a severe impact on the space around it and will affect what can be grown nearby. Beech is a notorious example, and its roots are near the surface too, so hardly anything will grow underneath. But you can avoid plunging your garden into gloom if you choose a tree with an upright (fastigiate) habit and/or one with light, fern-like foliage. There are quite a few good garden trees that fit the bill. Birches tend to have light, delicate foliage and are also quite narrow. Rowans *(Sorbus)* have slender, divided leaves and often an upright shape, so they don't cast much shade at all. Their berries come in various colours from pinkish white (*Sorbus hupehensis*) through orange and red (*Sorbus aucuparia* and *Sorbus commixta*) to golden (*Sorbus* 'Joseph Rock'). *Ginkgo* and *Gleditsia* cast light shade and are also worth considering, while for larger gardens, walnut, or ash or one of its cultivars, are very reliable. Both come into leaf late, casting little shade before midsummer – and by then you may be very glad of it. For a waterside setting in a small garden, the compact, willow-like tree *Pyrus salicifolia* 'Pendula' (*see* below) is an ideal choice. (*See also* pages 100–1.)

# Shrubs

As any garden design book will tell you, shrubs are the backbone of a garden, vital for providing permanent height and structure. Getting the right shrubs in the right places is critical to a successful planting scheme so choosing and siting them are big decisions. Fortunately, if you find you've made a mistake, most young shrubs can be moved successfully while they are dormant.

Different cultivars of dogwood offer a striking spectrum of winter stem colour – here, *Cornus alba* 'Sibirica', underplanted with snowdrops.

## Evergreen shrubs

Year-round structure in a garden usually relies on these, and they are also much used for screening, shelter and ground cover. Their main disadvantage is that, unlike their deciduous counterparts, most of them don't change much with the seasons, so it is best not to use too many together. But as a backdrop to other planting they are invaluable, and many of them are interesting enough to act as specimen plants, either in a border or in pots. Some, such as phormiums and yuccas (for a sunny place) or *Fatsia japonica* (for shade), are splendid architectural plants in their own right. Others, *Viburnum davidii* or *Osmanthus heterophyllus* for example, are reliable stalwarts that belong in the supporting cast. Many evergreens flower beautifully: you can grow rhododendrons and camellias in acid soil; ceanothus, cistus and hebe if you have sun and good drainage; mahonia and sarcococca for fragrant flowers to cheer you in winter.

## Deciduous shrubs

Many deciduous shrubs are also grown for their flowers. This is all very well for as long as the flowers last, but you will get much more value from your shrubs if you choose from the many multi-taskers that also contribute to the garden when they aren't in flower. Luckily this isn't

Surprisingly hardy, yuccas are among the boldest 'statement' shrubs.

difficult. Some – in particular certain popular dogwoods – have colourful winter bark. Others have been bred or selected by growers for their coloured foliage (*see* box, opposite). Then there are shrubs that produce spectacular autumn berries to keep you (or your garden birds) happy well into winter.

## Growing and pruning shrubs

Provided they are in a position and soil that suit them, and are properly watered and fed, most shrubs are easy to maintain. Many gardeners struggle with pruning, but remember that you aren't actually obliged to prune at all, and if you aren't sure it may be better to leave well alone. A basic knowledge of the whys and wherefores of pruning, however, is useful because you will then know how to tailor shrubs to the design of your garden, keeping them to the size and shape you want. So get to know the principles and you will soon understand why, when and how to prune.

### Controlling size and shape

It's usually best with shrubs to remove some branches completely each year. This benefits the plant, thinning the growth to let in air and light, and keeping the centre of the bush vigorous. Generally speaking, reserve light trimming for hedges and topiary. Most shrubs, if trimmed only lightly, will develop a surface covering of foliage and a dead, woody centre. They lose their individual character and look dull and artificial (not to say downright silly, in extreme cases).

## Encouraging growth and flowering

A grasp of basic pruning techniques will help you to get the best from your plants. Many shrubs, for example, need to be encouraged to keep producing new growth to perform well, and this is stimulated by pruning. Some shrubs flower better on new branches, so they need an annual pruning to keep them youthful and productive (buddleias, roses, caryopteris). Likewise, many shrubs grown for their foliage produce larger, brighter leaves on young growth (cotinus, ornamental elders). This will be at the expense of flowering, but the upside is a splendid foliage plant. Shrubs grown for colourful stems (certain dogwoods, and ornamental brambles such as *Rubus thibetanus*) have brighter bark colour on young wood. Some shrubs (daphnes, sarcococca and other naturally compact evergreens) need no pruning at all; others require removal of the oldest wood to keep them reasonably young at heart.

Removing some of the tired old wood from a weigela in autumn to promote vigorous new growth.

# Climbers

Climbers have a valuable role to play in all gardens, but they are especially useful for packing in interest and flower power where space is short. Grown over arches, arbours and pergolas they make wonderful garden features, adding height and seasonal colour (and often fragrance). You can train a climber up a pole or an obelisk for an attractive vertical focal point if there's no space for a tree, and in awkward spots it's possible to grow less vigorous climbers in containers.

## Climbers as planting partners

Some climbers are never happier than when scrambling through shrubs and up into trees, and they can even be planted in the same hole as long as food and water are plentiful. Clematis are ideal for this, as they like to flower in the sun but have their feet in the shade. A vigorous flowering shrub such as a forsythia or a large philadelphus is the perfect host, and the clematis flowers will stop the shrub from looking dreary in its 'off' season.

## Self-clinging climbers on walls

Areas of blank wall, especially in shade, cry out for planting to make them more interesting. Some plants have adhesive pads or aerial root hairs that enable them to climb up walls happily without you having to wobble about on a ladder, rigging up support for them. Provided the wall is perfectly sound, with no patches of crumbly mortar or render, self-clinging climbers such as ornamental ivies, *Euonymus fortunei* 'Silver Queen', or the climbing

Clematis – king of climbers. There is one for every situation and season. If you have room for only one, choose reliable, free-flowering forms such as *Clematis* 'Warszawska Nike', which produces its gorgeous velvety blooms over many weeks in summer and autumn.

Train climbing roses horizontally to encourage them to flower well.

hydrangea *Hydrangea anomala* subsp. *petiolaris* will do no harm to the structure. Keep them in check and prune them from time to time to keep them well away from gutters, windows and roof tiles. To get them started, fix the stems lightly to the wall with adhesive tape or Blu-Tack®, or hold them in place with the unobtrusive plastic fixings intended for electric and telephone cables. In dry weather, spray the wall with water from time to time to help the plant adhere.

Wisterias need a lot of space and a lot of pruning – but when they are in the right place, and well looked after, they're in a class of their own. This one has a perfect setting near the loggia at Wayford Manor, Somerset.

## Climbing roses

There's nothing like a climbing rose – especially if it's scented – to catch the mood of an old-fashioned country garden. Some of them have only a short flowering season, so partner them with another climber, such as a clematis or jasmine, to keep the interest going. For maximum flowering, train the rose so it makes a permanent framework of horizontal stems. The aim is to expose them to the sun, which will help them to ripen and flower well. Fix wires along a wall or fence; for a pillar, pergola or arbour train the young stems in a spiral round and round the post and then along the top of the structure. Tie them in with soft green or brown twine that won't cut into the soft stems as they grow, and trim off unwanted stems. Flowers will appear on side-shoots, and should be dead-headed as soon as they fade – some go brown and continue to cling to the shoots, spoiling the display. Reliable, fragrant climbers include: *Rosa* 'Compassion' (peach-pink) *below top*, *R.* 'Golden Showers' (yellow) and *R.* 'Madame Alfred Carrière' (pink-tinged white) *below bottom*.

## Some climbers for pergolas

■ *Clematis* 'Huldine' The pearly-white flowers of this vigorous and sun-loving summer-flowering clematis look best when viewed from below with the sun behind to show up their attractive pinkish undersides – so it's perfect for pergolas. *C.* 'Huldine' is also a good companion for roses, honeysuckle and other climbers. Cut the plant hard back in late winter for the best display the following summer.

■ *Cobaea scandens* This tender annual is a good bet for a new pergola in its first year, while you wait for permanent planting to establish. If you sow seed in early spring and keep the plants frost-free until the weather is warm enough to plant them out, they will race away, and by late summer your pergola will be dripping with subtle purple bell-shaped flowers that will last until autumn frosts.

■ *Rosa* 'Adélaïde d'Orléans' Good foliage, abundant creamy-white flowers and lax stems that are easy to tie in make this delicately fragrant old-fashioned rambler rose a good plant for a romantic pergola. It combines well with blue or purple clematis such as the free-flowering *Clematis* 'Étoile Violette' or the old favourite *C.* 'Jackmanii'.

■ *Wisteria sinensis* A good wisteria can turn a large, stout pergola or a spacious house wall into a classic set-piece for a traditional garden. Its plentiful, fragrant, hanging flower trusses are a delight to sit under in early summer, and the foliage stays attractive all season. Wisteria buds break quite late, which means they don't blot out too much spring sunshine but you have the benefit of shade when you really need it, in midsummer. Make sure the pergola is tall enough for the hanging flowers to be above head height, and be prepared for a vigorous pruning job twice a year when the plant is mature. Wisterias on a house wall should be tied in to horizontal wires secured by vine eyes fixed into the wall.

*See also* pages 104–5.

# Herbaceous perennials

This is the most versatile plant group in the garden designer's palette, offering long-lasting plants for every season, purpose, colour scheme and mood. Whether you are looking for an elegant 'statement' plant or ground cover, something to feed the birds in winter or a reliable source of cut flowers for the house, there will always be a herbaceous perennial to fit the bill.

## What are herbaceous perennials?

Strictly speaking, all plants that go on from year to year, including shrubs and trees, are perennials. Among gardeners in temperate climates, however, the terms 'herbaceous plant' and 'perennial' are used to mean non-woody plants with stems and leaves that die back to ground level in autumn, leaving a rootstock that remains alive to produce new growth next year.

## Using perennials

The herbaceous border, that stalwart of the English garden, has become rather a thing of the past, with its need for high maintenance to keep it looking its best through many months of the year. In its place we have the mixed border, which is a much more practical, varied and long-lasting tapestry of plants of different kinds, with interest for every season. Herbaceous perennials play an important part in this kind of

Check over your herbaceous perennials in early spring, dividing any congested clumps like this kniphofia. Re-plant small healthy pieces in improved soil.

planting, complementing shrubs, bulbs and perhaps annuals too, in a variety of ways. They provide reliable 'furnishing' for the spaces between, or in front of, shrubs, and at ground level they disguise the dying foliage of spring bulbs and keep the soil covered to discourage weeds and retain moisture. They provide seasonal accents of colour from spring to autumn, many of them have interesting foliage, and some have attractive, architectural skeletons that will enhance the garden over winter, remaining in place until cut down in spring.

A planting design always looks stronger if you use groups of plants rather than single ones, and this applies particularly to perennials. It is often recommended that they are planted in groups of three or five. In many cases it's easy to increase your stock by splitting clumps up (see photograph above), and in this way you will have a supply that enables you to repeat groups of your tried and tested favourites in different places. Such deliberate repetition will help to give coherence and unity to your planting scheme.

## Growing perennials

Most perennials are relatively easy to grow in reasonable soil, and as there is such a wide choice, if one plant doesn't seem to like your garden it won't be difficult to find something broadly similar to try instead. The pot-grown perennials you find in garden centres can be planted at any time of year, provided they are watered well if the weather is dry.

Maintenance is fairly light if you steer clear of perennials that are too vigorous and remember to stake tall plants, such as delphiniums, early in the season. Work through each border once a year – early spring is a good time – so you can split up clumps that are getting too large, or that are dying off in the middle. Simply lift the clump and either pull

Perennials aren't just for summer. This dark hellebore, a choice late winter flower, is a very good partner for snowdrops.

it apart into individual crowns or chop it vertically into pieces with a sharp spade, making sure that each little clump has some healthy young shoots emerging from it. Refresh the soil by adding some compost, and replant the best divisions. Keep the border weed-free: mulching with compost or fine chipped bark in winter or early spring will help with this, and feed the plants too. The only other requirement is that you cut down the stems after flowering. This keeps the border looking fresh, and will also encourage some perennials to flower again.

## Star performers

Easy but interesting to propagate, herbaceous perennials have long attracted the passion of enthusiasts up and down the land. As a result there are literally thousands of different cultivars to choose from. Some plant groups, such as hostas, peonies, heucheras, irises and daylilies, could single-handedly fill several gardens, such is the bewildering variety of different forms. Some of these are almost indistinguishable from one another, but others really stand out from the crowd. In designing gardens it's invaluable to get to know the forms that are 'good doers' because these will really earn their space, while others, however beautiful, may grow half-heartedly and never make a real impact. A good guide to the best performers is the RHS Award of Garden Merit (*see* box). This award scheme applies to all plants, not just perennials, but it is particularly useful for telling the sheep from the goats in this very large group.

### A dozen 'good doers'

*Acanthus spinosus*
*Achillea filipendulina* 'Gold Plate'
*Anemone* x *hybrida* 'Honorine Jobert'
*Aster* x *frikartii* 'Mönch' (below bottom)
*Euphorbia characias* subsp. *wulfenii*
*Geranium psilostemon*
*Geranium* 'Rozanne'
*Hemerocallis* 'Corky'
*Iris sibirica* 'Butter and Sugar'
*Penstemon* 'Andenken an Friedrich Hahn'
*Pulmonaria* 'Lewis Palmer'
*Sedum* 'Herbstfreude' (below top)

### The Award of Garden Merit (AGM)

This scheme is operated by the Royal Horticultural Society (RHS) to help identify the best plants for all-round value in the garden. The award is given to certain plants after RHS assessment and trials have shown them to be of good constitution, easy to grow, and not too susceptible to pests and diseases. AGM plants are identified by a special 'cup' symbol ♀, sometimes used on plant labels, and all can be found in the *RHS Plant Finder*, which is available online or annually in book form.

# Annuals and biennials

Among the best sources of bright summer colour, annuals and biennials can be relied upon to keep the show going when perennials are taking time out. These wonderful seed-grown plants include many old garden favourites – foxgloves, forget-me-nots, poppies, wallflowers, marigolds and sweet peas – as well as plants that produce some of the most attractive seedheads, such as honesty and love-in-a-mist (*see also* pages 124–5). Short-lived they may be, but gardens simply wouldn't be the same without them.

Love-in-a-mist (*Nigella damascena*) is one of those useful, welcome self-seeding annuals that pop up unexpectedly every year, yet it is seldom in the wrong place. Its seed-heads are as pretty as its flowers.

## Growing annuals and biennials

This large category is divided into several groups for growing purposes. Hardy and half-hardy annuals usually grow from seed, flower, produce seed, and die – all in the same year. Biennials take two, or even three, growing seasons for the same process. And sometimes certain tender perennials are treated as annuals, since they are invariably killed by autumn frosts.

Hardy annuals can be sown outdoors where they are to flower, either in spring or in some cases in autumn, to get a head start. Some of them self-seed once established, leaving you to remove any surplus self-sown seedlings (*see* page 35). Half-hardy annuals are so called because they can't stand cold weather. Sow them in pots and bring them on in a frost-free place, gradually hardening them off so you can plant out after the last frost.

Biennials such as sweet williams and wallflowers are often sown in the vegetable plot in early summer, then thinned and grown on until autumn, when they should be big enough to move to the flower bed. Again, some of them – foxgloves and honesty for example – are adept self-sowers. You can always move the seedlings to where you want them to flower (although they will often have a better idea).

## Using annuals

Some annuals, such as cosmos, zinnias and antirrhinums, will soon

Sarah Raven's cutting garden at Perch Hill in spring. Wallflowers – biennials grown from seed the previous year – provide colour and fragrance for garden and house.

make large, statuesque plants that are ideal for filling the gaps when early perennials have finished. Plant breeders are producing more and more dwarf versions of familiar annuals, which are good for patio pots, but in mixed borders it is best to go for larger plants, and fewer of them, as this looks more natural. Some gardeners still enjoy 'bedding out' – using nothing but annuals in the style of old-fashioned public parks – to create the traditional 'riot of colour' from early summer until the first frosts.

## Using biennials

Biennials such as forget-me-nots and wallflowers (traditionally grown with

Early summer annuals and biennials at Perch Hill (see opposite): Iceland poppies (*Papaver nudicaule*), California poppies (*Eschscholzia californica*) and white foxgloves.

tulips) can also be used for bedding, neatly filling the period after earlier spring bulbs have finished. Sweet williams are good for cutting, too, and they look great in rows – brightening a vegetable garden or featuring in a dedicated cutting garden. Foxgloves, honesty, sweet rocket and other more informal biennials are good for wild areas, or to precede summer perennials in a border, where their lush late-spring foliage will conveniently mask the unsightly leaves of dying bulbs.

### Don't forget

Plants of many kinds bloom for longer if their spent flowerheads are removed, but dead-heading is particularly important in prolonging the life of annuals such as sweet peas, marigolds and petunias. An annual plant's aim in life is to flower and set seed to reproduce itself, but if you frustrate its attempts to do this by removing dead flowers, seeds can't form, and it will just keep on trying by continuing to throw out new flowers.

### Climbers from seed

Annuals that climb make quick, colourful cover for garden structures such as arches and pergolas while you wait for permanent planting to mature and take their place. They are useful for creating height in a border, trained up a decorative obelisk or an informal wigwam of tall twigs. Sweet peas and nasturtiums are probably the most familiar annual climbers, but several others are readily available such as *Cobaea scandens*, morning glory (*see* page 93) – a sun-lover that produces beautiful sky-blue trumpets every morning in late summer – and Canary creeper, with its unusual toothed yellow flowers. Climbers such as the Chilean glory flower *Eccremocarpus scaber* (below) or the flamboyant *Ipomoea lobata*, are ideal for an (almost) instant touch of the exotic, with their hot colours, quick growth and enthusiastic response to a warm summer.

# Bulbs

Bulbs take some beating. They're colourful, economical on space, easy to grow and relatively cheap. They give quick results and may well go on for years, multiplying to make a dazzling seasonal impact, with plenty left over to lift and plant elsewhere in your garden or pass on to your friends and relations. The most familiar bulbs flower in spring, and colour is never more welcome than at this time. But don't neglect the more unusual ones that flower later in the year.

Tulips and wallflowers are a classic pairing – here, *Tulipa* 'Dillenburg' with *Erysimum latifolium*.

## Bulbs in borders

Many spring bulbs make perfect partners for herbaceous plants in borders, providing cheerful colour amidst the young foliage of the awakening perennials. But when you're thinking about what to partner with what, do consider how the bulbs will look when they have just finished flowering and are at their tattiest. Eventually, of course, they will become dormant and you can forget about them until next season, but in the meantime how do you avoid having to look at their unlovely dying leaves? Whatever you do, don't cut them off yet. It's fine to pick off the dead flowerheads, but the fading leaves and stem will

The season's barely started, but with cyclamen, chionodoxas and hellebores there's no shortage of colour.

feed and fatten the bulb so it can flower again next year. A good tip is to partner bulbs with a deciduous shrub or a perennial that will be coming into strong growth just in time to hide the dying foliage. If you're clever you can arrange it so that the new leaves of the companion plant complement the bulbs' flowers – try orange tulips with a purple elder (*Sambucus nigra* 'Eva') or the dark-leaved *Geranium pratense* 'Black Beauty'; or partner deep blue hyacinths, *Anemone blanda* or scillas with golden-leaved plants – for example *Philadelphus coronarius* 'Aureus'.

## Bulbs in grass

Big daffodils are usually the first victims of spring gales and rains. Even if they come through those unscathed, they look messy for weeks after flowering and you find yourself itching to mow them down

The delicate snakeshead fritillary (*Fritillaria meleagris*) – wonderful for naturalizing in damp grassland.

too soon. Instead, go for a low, carpeting effect, with drifts of the smaller varieties of narcissi and other early-flowering little bulbs, which will shine jewel-like in the early spring sunshine, then die off politely without causing any untidiness. Many will self-sow over the years, creating a natural-looking tapestry in the grass. Crocuses are a familiar example but the petals open only when the sun shines, and the birds and mice do love them. *Anemone blanda* – blue, white or pink – makes quite an impression and has pretty, ferny foliage. For a reliable haze of blue in any weather, even in partial shade, choose one of the various kinds of scilla and chionodoxa.

To give your little spring bulbs the best possible setting, keep mowing until late autumn so the grass is short enough not to drown them when they're in flower. If you need to mow in winter, remember to avoid the areas where the bulbs are.

## Bulbs in containers

A packet of bulbs planted in an attractive pot will probably cost you less than a bunch of flowers and is certain to last longer. Feed and keep them watered for a while after flowering, and many kinds will give you a second or third year's display without repotting.

Pots of bulbs near doorways or just outside windows are lovely at any time of year. They can be put in place at just the right moment for you to enjoy the flowers as they open, then replaced with something else when past their best. For late winter try *Cyclamen coum*, early varieties of snowdrop or *Iris*

### Autumn-flowering bulbs

■ *Colchicum speciosum* 'Album' Huge pure white goblets make this a truly choice plant. Partner it, and all colchicums, with something to disguise the conspicuous leaves as they die off in spring.

■ *Colchicum* 'Waterlily' There's nothing to match this exotic double-flowered pink starlet if the weather is kind and the setting right.

■ *Crocus speciosus* Similar to their spring counterparts, these lavender crocuses are a welcome surprise when they suddenly flower, usually after a spell of early autumn rain.

■ *Cyclamen hederifolium* Tolerant of surprisingly harsh conditions, these easiest of cyclamens have lovely marbled foliage for months after they flower, so they're hugely valuable in winter. Look for the curious, curly seedheads, too.

■ *Nerine bowdenii* Large sugar-pink, frilly flowers in late autumn aren't what you expect. This sun-loving bulb is unrivalled for late-season 'wow factor' against a warm wall.

■ *Sternbergia lutea* Yellow crocus-like flowers to brighten autumn days make this slightly tricky plant worth growing if you can get it to flower. It likes light soil and dislikes overcrowding, so split up the clumps from time to time.

'Harmony' in a warm, sunny place. A little later come the early, bright miniature daffodils such as *Narcissus* 'Tête-à-tête' or *Narcissus* 'Jack Snipe'. For a wider range of colours, choose hyacinths or tulips, generously planted in groups of at least 10 or 15, to fill the container. Pack them in closely for greater effect, but don't let the bulbs quite touch each other.

For summer pots, tubs and borders there are lilies (such as fragrant *Lilium regale*), gladioli, and the remarkable *Galtonia candicans*, a sort of tall, white, summer-flowering hyacinth. When planting bulbs in containers, choose large ones filled with a soil-based compost so they don't get top-heavy.

# Screening

For a garden to be the secluded haven of your dreams, it must at least create the illusion of being a place apart, a beautiful retreat where the outside world seems far away. Your outdoor space can be enclosed by fences and hedges up to a certain height, but you may need to adopt specific tactics when you want to blot out taller intrusive features.

### Screening with trees

A thoughtfully positioned tree can be ideal for screening, but first there are careful choices to be made. You don't want to wait patiently for the tree to be tall enough to do its job, only to wish you'd chosen something else.

Think twice before you plant an evergreen tree to make your garden more private. Sometimes, when you have a difficult screening problem to solve, evergreens are the only answer, but they do have their disadvantages.

Mature evergreen trees block out not only the unwanted views but also the sky and the sunlight, all year round, and they severely limit what you can grow beneath their canopy. Some evergreens look much the same all year, so choose one that will offer seasonal variety. This might include berries (holly or yew), catkins (evergreen oak) or interesting cones (*Abies koreana*). *Prunus lusitanica*, the Portugal laurel, is mostly seen as a shrub or hedging plant, but it makes a good bushy tree, laden with fragrant, fluffy cream flower spikes in late spring. *Arbutus unedo*, the strawberry tree, is unusual in having flowers and fruits at the same time, with attractive bark as a further bonus.

Often a deciduous tree is a better bet, letting in precious sunshine in winter when privacy in the garden

Plants for screening. ① The black stems of *Phyllostachys nigra* make a good feature in contemporary gardens. ② *Prunus cerasifera* 'Nigra' blossoms early in the year. ③ Yew hedging topped with a rambler rose makes a secluded retreat.

## Trees and shrubs for screening

*Ceanothus* 'Concha'
*Crataegus* x *lavalleei* 'Carrierei' (below)
*Crataegus persimilis* 'Prunifolia'
*Phyllostachys nigra*
*Prunus cerasifera*

may be less important, while giving welcome shade and leaf cover in summer. However, some trees, such as apple, walnut or ash, come into leaf relatively late, while others, such as horse-chestnut, lose their leaves early in the autumn. If screening is important, choose something that has a long season of leaf cover, or that blossoms before the leaves open, extending the tree's season of useful screening. Think about the shape of the tree, too. One with a low, spreading canopy may give better protection from a neighbouring window (though it will cast more shade), while a tall, slender tree (*see* page 105) may be more effective in blotting out an eyesore such as a phone mast without excluding too much light.

### Structures for screening

Even for the most patient, there may come a time when you need some screening and you need it *now*. This often happens when an extension or new building springs up on a neighbouring plot, and you suddenly lose your view or are overlooked by new windows. Buying mammoth shrubs and trees to restore calm is certainly possible, but they will cost an arm and a leg (and a lot of grey hairs worrying about whether they are going to establish successfully). A pergola or trellis may be a much better option, giving a measure of screening straightaway, with cover improving all the time as plants grow to clothe it. To prevent a seating area from being overlooked by an upstairs window, an overhead pergola with the beams set fairly close together is probably the best solution.

### Don't forget

If you are trying to block out something large, always position screening, such as trellis panels, close to your own viewpoint – rather than immediately in front of the offending object.

### Shrubs as trees

Plant a shrub that will grow big enough to hide an unsightly feature, and it takes up half your flower border. Plant a tree, and you may well find that within a few years you have blocked out not only your neighbour's washing, as intended, but also your sunshine and your view. The choice of trees that can easily be kept compact is limited, but some shrubs can be pruned to behave like trees. Just remove the side shoots gradually, from the bottom up, as the plant grows. That way you have the best of both worlds: your privacy, and planting space underneath. Try it with these:

■ *Cornus mas* Very early, delicate golden flowers in spring, and good autumn leaf colour, make this an asset to any garden. The variegated form is worth finding if you can.

■ *Cotinus coggygria* Any variety of this familiar foliage shrub makes a good bronze- or purple-leaved specimen as a shrub or small tree.

■ *Euonymus* Spindles such as *Euonymus europaeus* and *Euonymus planipes* make nice little trees with good autumn colour, and the curious fruits can be seen near eye level.

■ *Sambucus* There is a whole range of ornamental elders – variegated, cut-leaved, golden and purple – with one for every planting scheme. They are usually pruned hard to encourage vigorous foliage, but they will make a decent tree if you remove young shoots from the base of the plant.

■ *Viburnum rhytidophyllum* Usually seen as an enormous, rather dull shrub, this evergreen comes into its own as a multi-stemmed tree, exposing the felted undersides of the bold, crinkly leaves as well as the attractive russet bark. Its striking swags of shiny red and black berries are anything but dull, but it needs a partner to bear fruit.

Climbers creating cover. ① A climber such as this white-flowered solanum will make a living 'roof', providing shade and privacy for alfresco dining. ② Just standing under a pergola clad with the vigorous and reliable *Clematis* 'Perle d'Azur' is pure joy.

# Hedges

Versatile, long-lived and beneficial to wildlife, a well-planted hedge is a joy forever – well, for quite a long time. Planting hedges involves a short spell of hard work and then a degree of patience while they get established, but the end result will justify the investment many times over. Whether you want a simple screen or a thorny barrier – plant a hedge.

The base of a hedge can be a 'dead space', where weeds can easily gain a foothold. The problem has been solved here with a planting of trouble-free purple dog violets (*Viola riviniana* Purpurea Group).

## Plants for hedging

■ *Buxus sempervirens* (box) Less popular than it used to be owing to the increasingly widespread disease box blight, box has always been one of the traditional plants for formal evergreen hedges, and it is very good in shade. A slow-growing form, *Buxus sempervirens* 'Suffruticosa', is the classic dwarf hedging used to edge beds, and for knot gardens. It's very easy to root from cuttings if you need a lot of it. When buying box, first inspect the plants closely and look out for leaves that have turned brown, a symptom of box blight. With established box, sometimes whole branches die off, especially in damp weather. Cut off affected parts and burn them. *Euonymus japonicus* 'Microphyllus' is a good substitute.

■ *Fagus sylvatica* (beech) Though deciduous, beech hedging provides cover for most of the year, keeping its dead leaves until early spring. It is lovely when the fresh green leaves break a few weeks later. *Carpinus* *betulus* (hornbeam) is similar to beech, but better in heavy soil.

■ *Ilex crenata* 'Convexa' You would probably never guess, but this is a kind of holly. Tiny, rounded evergreen leaves and small black berries make it look more like box, and – if you can find it – it is a good alternative hedging.

■ *Lonicera nitida* This familiar small-leaved evergreen works well for hedges up to about 1.2m (4ft) but tends to flop if you let it get much higher. It grows fast and needs clipping once a month in summer. If it gets out of hand, it will respond to hard cutting back.

■ *Phillyrea angustifolia* A bushy broadleaved evergreen, related to the olive, this is another good alternative to box if box blight is a problem (*see Buxus*, left).

■ *Taxus baccata* (yew) This is the king of hedging, and not as slow-growing as people think. It makes a sleek, dark green, slender hedge – a flattering formal backdrop for any planting scheme – and it only needs

Copper beech is excellent if you want a hedge that changes with the seasons. The young foliage, almost coral, gradually settles to a deep bronze-purple, which gives way to russet tones in winter.

clipping once a year (late summer is best). It can usually be renovated by cutting back, however old the plants. Two disadvantages: it isn't good on very damp soil, and it is poisonous to livestock.

■ *Thuja plicata* (western red cedar) This makes an attractive evergreen hedge rather similar in style to the notoriously rampant leylandii (x *Cupressocyparis leylandii*) but more manageable. Unlike leylandii it will re-sprout after cutting back if it becomes too large. It needs clipping twice a year, once in spring and again in late summer.

## Sshhh!

Unless you have hedges of enormous size, try to clip them with hand shears rather than a power trimmer. Tackle the job in two or three sessions if it seems like hard work, but for the average garden hedge, light, sharp, modern shears aren't arduous to use and they are much less antisocial – and greener – than the noisy (and often unnecessary) alternative. They also give a cleaner cut, reducing the risk of introducing disease through crushed plant tissue. And you'll be able to hear the birds singing while you do it.

## Restoring a hedge

You can renovate old, thin or misshapen hedges of native plants such as yew, hawthorn, holly, privet and hazel with good results. Cut back one side at a time over two winters (spring is better for evergreens) and you will have a good, thick hedge again far sooner than if you had planted from scratch. Many conifers, such as the giant x *Cupressocyparis leylandii* and the similar *Chamaecyparis lawsoniana*, will not tolerate hard pruning at all, and it's better to remove them if they have got out of hand.

## HOW TO plant a hedge

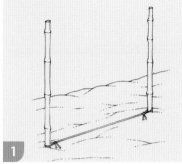

**1** Order bare-rooted hedging plants of your chosen variety. Plant on a dry day from late autumn to early spring when the soil isn't frozen or waterlogged. Begin by stretching a line between two or more posts to mark the position of the hedge.

**2** Dig a trench about 30cm (12in) deep and wide, breaking up the soil at the bottom with a fork. Add compost and a slow-release fertilizer to the soil you have just removed and then also to the base of the trench.

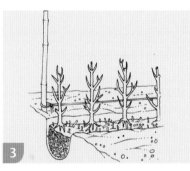

**3** Space the plants along the line in a single row, 30–50cm (12–20in) apart. For a very high hedge the plants will need more room to grow, so give each one enough space by setting them out in a staggered row farther apart – up to 60cm (24in).

**4** Fill in the trench with the mixture of topsoil and compost, firm with your foot, and water in well to settle the roots. To encourage the new hedge to thicken from the base, cut all the plants back to 15cm (6in) after planting.

## Native hedging

Gardeners and farmers are now choosing to plant mixed native hedges because they are so good for wildlife. These hedges provide nesting sites and winter berries for birds, and habitats for insects, as well as interest for people. Native hedging is usually bought as small, inexpensive bare-rooted plants in winter, when they are dormant. You can buy these by mail order – look in gardening magazines or online – and plant immediately unless the ground is frozen. Typical species might include:

*Acer campestre* (field maple)
*Cornus sanguinea* (dogwood)
*Crataegus monogyna* (hawthorn)
*Euonymus europaeus* (spindle)
*Ligustrum vulgare* (wild privet)
*Prunus spinosa* (blackthorn)
*Rhamnus cathartica* (buckthorn)
*Viburnum lantana* (wayfaring tree)
*Viburnum opulus* (guelder rose)

# Creating height

The third dimension, height, is sometimes neglected in garden design, but without it a garden can so easily be flat and dull. It's important to include taller features, whether plants or structures, to give the garden more variety and a sense of scale. Vertical growing also increases your available planting space and creates lots of opportunities for extra plant colour and interest.

## Pergolas

A plant-covered pergola is one of the most effective design devices you can add to a garden to create height. It can also fulfil other design functions: giving a sense of enclosure to a seating area, or a strong feeling of direction if it spans a path; adding a focal point or a full stop; blotting out an unwanted view; linking a house with its garden; or blurring the distinction between man-made structure and natural planting. (*See also* pages 50, 66–7.)

## Arbours

Usually an intimate structure clothed with climbing plants and sheltering a seat, an arbour is a very traditional concept, harking back to romantic trysts in medieval gardens. Arbours are usually constructed from metal or wood – normally timber, either rustic or sawn – but sometimes from living willow or woven hurdles, or even carved out of an evergreen hedge. An arbour offers great scope for creativity and originality, in the structure itself and in the plants you use to furnish it. Beautiful and functional in both traditional and contemporary settings, arbours work perfectly in even the smallest garden, both as a secluded retreat that defines a separate little space and as an inviting focal point.

## Arches

An arch is used to frame an entrance, leading into the garden itself perhaps, or from one part of it to another.

Arches should be positioned where they will create an element of surprise – what lies beyond? A freestanding arch in the middle of a garden never looks quite right. Use it in tandem with an opening in a hedge or fence, a door or gateway, or a gap in the planting to either side of it, and it will make much more sense. An arch can also be used to frame a mirror to give the illusion of more space, but this trick does need to be staged very carefully to be effective, and is essential to have plenty of planting around it to distract the eye from the mechanics.

## Obelisks

An obelisk is a versatile, incidental means of creating height – either as a single focal point or as one of a series. An obelisk is a reasonably quick way of giving scale and shape to a border where a tree would create unwanted shade or be too dominant. Obelisks can be solid or open, and may or may not support climbing plants. In a small garden an obelisk can be a valuable means of emphasizing height, especially if clothed with greenery, without using much lateral space. An obelisk as a plant support can be used to top a large container, planted with a flowering climber, or with clipped ivy or box for a more formal effect.

A tree can eventually be a host for climbers such as roses and clematis ① – but will require patience. An obelisk ② is a better option where height and structure are needed quickly.

## Plants for adding height

SLENDER TREES
*Carpinus betulus* 'Fastigiata'
*Fagus sylvatica* 'Dawyck'
*Prunus* 'Spire'
*Pyrus calleryana* 'Chanticleer'
*Sorbus aucuparia* 'Fastigiata'

UPRIGHT SHRUBS
*Berberis thunbergii* f. *atropurpurea* 'Helmond Pillar'
*Buddleja davidii* 'Black Knight'
*Ilex aquifolium* 'Pyramidalis'
*Juniperus communis* 'Hibernica'
*Mahonia* x *media* cultivars
*Phyllostachys nigra*
*Rosa* 'Geranium'
*Taxus baccata* 'Fastigiata'

Tall and slender plants. ① *Taxus baccata* 'Fastigiata' and ② *Fagus sylvatica* 'Dawyck Purple'. For vertical emphasis in a border, try perennials such as *Verbena bonariensis* and *Crocosmia* 'Lucifer' ③.

### Poles

This simple means of supporting a climber is also a cheap and effective way of creating height. The pole needs to be stout, made of either hardwood or pressure-treated softwood, and well anchored into the ground. Stain it black if you want it to be unobtrusive. Then plant a climber such as a clematis, honeysuckle or climbing rose at its foot, tying it in as it grows.

### Vertical planting

More than any other single feature, a tree makes a real difference to a garden, providing its own unique combination of height, shade, restful greenery and wildlife habitat. You should never need to ask yourself whether you should plant a tree in your garden, even if it is a small space. As long as you've done your homework and choose wisely, the answer will always be yes, and more than one if space allows. A number of tree cultivars tend to have an upright shape (*see* box) and are worth considering if space is at a premium.

In a border, if you are seeking height without bulk, there are several obliging shrubs (*see* box), or you could grow a climber on a pole or obelisk. There are also many herbaceous plants and grasses that have a clear emphasis on the vertical (*see also* page 82). Foxgloves, lupins, verbascums and *Eremurus* (foxtail lilies) have colourful, upright flower spikes, while good cultivars of *Calamagrostis* and *Miscanthus* are useful tall grasses with a relatively small footprint.

# Vegetables by design

Now that kitchen gardening has become quite – well – chic, it's strange to think that not so many years ago vegetables were regarded as the poor relations of the garden. In grand gardens they were hidden away as though they were a real blot on the landscape, far from the house and preferably in a walled enclosure so they didn't spoil the view. Now, thank goodness, all that has changed. Your own fresh, tasty organically grown vegetables form an integral part of the garden and are something to be really proud of.

A well-planned vegetable garden needn't be sophisticated. Simple, timber-edged raised beds are an easy way to start. Don't forget to include a place to sit and admire your crops.

Inspired colour scheming in the potager at West Green House. The palette here includes runner beans, red brassicas, sweet peas and *Cerinthe major* 'Purpurascens'.

## A kitchen garden

Vegetable growing can be highly decorative, as in the classic potager, but you don't need an acre and a crack team of garden designers to plan your vegetable patch with an artistic eye. Even if you don't go for the all-out ornamental approach, don't neglect design concerns at the planning stage. As with any other piece of garden design, start with a good framework and strong lines. A kitchen garden must, above all, be practical. Sunshine, easy access and good soil are essential, and you will need water (butts or a tap) and compost bins close by. A cold frame for seedlings is also worth finding room for, if you can. Many successful vegetable growers use a system of intensive, dedicated beds. These can be raised (*see* page 43) or at ground level, with or without an edging of timber, bricks, stones, tiles, miniature hurdles, plants or anything you fancy. The soil in the beds should be cultivated to a good depth and improved with lots of compost at the outset.

Whatever the shape of the beds, and whether they are edged or not, keep them narrow so that you can reach the middle from either side without stepping on the soil, to avoid compaction. This means a maximum width of about 1.2m (4ft). Plants in these beds can be grown closer together, leaving less scope for weeds; and instead of arduous winter digging every year you just fork over the soil between successive crops and spread more compost on the beds.

The permanent paths in between can be made from compacted earth, grass, old bricks or paving slabs, shingle or chipped bark. Paths don't need to be very wide, normally

You can create an attractively designed composition with vegetable plants even in a tiny space. Here, chillies of different colours and shapes, in pots in a sunny courtyard.

## Potagers

If you want to take your kitchen garden into a different league, you can create a potager or ornamental kitchen garden. There are some very beautiful and ambitious examples to visit for inspiration, but a small back-garden potager can simply be an appealing arrangement of beds and paths, built with pleasing materials and thoughtfully planted with a mixture of vegetables, fruit, herbs and flowers. A seating area, perhaps with some plants in attractive pots, is a bonus, and the potager will feel even more satisfactory if you add permanent height in the form of trained soft fruit, well-maintained espalier fruit trees or a vine pergola.

## Good companions

Cottage gardeners of old often mixed vegetables, herbs and fruit with flowers in the garden. Whereas for them it was usually a question of adding flowers to the vegetable patch, which provided much of their basic food, in today's small gardens we are more likely to be squeezing a few vegetables into our flower borders. This can work well. The dense planting helps keep the soil moist and weed-free, and growing a mixture of plants together helps to control pests and diseases. As with flower borders, plan interesting combinations of different colours, shapes and textures. Below, globe artichokes are backed by foxgloves and *Rosa* x *odorata* 'Mutabilis'. Catmint lines the path.

50–60cm (20–24in) will be enough, but you may like to make at least one main path of 90cm (3ft), which will be wide enough to negotiate with a full wheelbarrow.

## Planning your planting

At the start of each season it's worth spending time planning where your crops are to go. Make a note of where you plant each crop each year, setting up a system of rotation to get the best out of your soil and prevent a build-up of crop-specific pests and diseases. Within that, consider what is most convenient. For example, vegetables that need frequent watering could be positioned close to a water butt. The ones you'll be picking more or less daily, such as beans, courgettes or tomatoes, could be next to a path, and herbs such as parsley and chives close to the kitchen for hurried forays when you're cooking.

## Crop protection

Vegetable crops attract a range of notorious pests, from aphids to wood pigeons. You can keep many of these unwelcome visitors away by covering your crops, but modern crop-protection materials can be unattractive and hard to disguise in an ornamental garden.

A bed system enables you to cover each bed individually – with cloches, fleece, netting or whatever is appropriate – at vulnerable times. Use black fruit-cage netting to keep pigeons, sparrows and blackbirds off their favourite targets: brassicas, peas, beetroot, ripening strawberries and many more. If you stretch netting taut over a neatly made framework of canes or hoops, its visual impact will be minimal. Reflective materials such as foil or unwanted CDs, hung from string so that they flash and twinkle in the wind, are a temporary deterrent. Traditional solutions include an old-fashioned scarecrow – doubling as

a garden sculpture – or thorny twigs pushed into the ground to deter birds, cats and other animals. Companion planting, which many gardeners swear by, is a decorative way to keep certain pests at bay.

# The prettiest vegetables?

While kitchen gardening enthusiasts would stoutly maintain that all vegetables are beautiful, it would be fair to say that, as ornamental plants, some have more going for them than others. This may be partly to do with how easy it is to keep them looking smart. Below is a selection of vegetables – some for each season – that will hold their own in an ornamental garden, be it a potager or a flower border.

**BEANS  Summer**  Climbing beans score points because they lend valuable height to a garden scheme and can be grown on ornamental structures such as obelisks. They also have colour, from runner beans with scarlet or scarlet-and-white flowers, to climbing French beans with golden or purple pods.

**BEETROOT  Summer/autumn**
Beetroot is a good dual-purpose vegetable, useful for its young leaves, which are decorative and tasty in salads, and for its roots, of course. Purple beets are familiar but there are also orange varieties.

**BRASSICAS  Winter**  Well-grown plants of a mixture of brassicas – red cabbage, Brussels sprouts, purple-sprouting broccoli and crinkly black Tuscan kale – can provide interest all winter. To look attractive the plants must be in tip-top condition, so feed them well, stake if necessary, and keep one step ahead of the caterpillars and pigeons.

The cherry tomato 'Gardener's Delight' is a favourite with many gardeners – it's prolific, early to ripen, and always reliably sweet.

scheme. Taller, cordon varieties can be supported by an attractive fence. Like runner beans, tomatoes were originally introduced as decorative plants, not for eating. Different colours are available: red, golden, pink and purple.

Unusual kinds of beetroot to try include 'Chioggia', an old Italian variety that when sliced reveals concentric pink and white rings.

Purple-sprouting broccoli helps furnish the kitchen garden all through winter, with delicious shoots to look forward to in spring.

**CHERRY TOMATOES  Summer**
Always tempting, bush varieties can be planted in containers, positioned symmetrically to enhance a formal

One for those who don't like their chillies too scorching, 'Hungarian Hot Wax' is a good, easily obtainable variety with large, showy fruits.

## CHILLIES AND OTHER PEPPERS

**Summer** Healthy-looking, shiny ripe chillies of different shapes, sizes, colours and hotness lend excitement to any patio or greenhouse and, given enough warmth and shelter, they are very easy to grow. There are over 200 varieties around – why not try one of each!

## CHIVES **Spring** One of the first

edible treats of the year, chives emerge in early spring as fresh green shoots, and a couple of months later produce pretty pinkish-mauve edible flowers that look wonderful sprinkled on top of salads.

## GLOBE ARTICHOKES **Spring and summer** Very similar to the

cardoon, a globe artichoke plant has such presence that you can forgive it

Growing your own globe artichokes brings a touch of class to both garden and kitchen – and they aren't difficult, once established.

for looking a bit tatty after the crop is harvested. Avoid leaving stumps when you cut the artichokes, and leave some of the smaller ones to flower, both to prolong the season and to please the bees.

## LEEKS **Autumn and winter** An

invaluable kitchen standby, leeks add an architectural touch to the garden all winter, particularly if planted symmetrically.

## ONIONS AND GARLIC **Summer**

Like leeks, these are pleasing to look at if well grown and neatly planted. They make a good vertical contrast with more sprawling vegetables.

## PARSLEY **All year** Perhaps the

most useful kitchen herb to have freshly available, parsley is a feast for the eyes, especially if you feed and water it well. The curly-leaved variety has a froth of bright green leaves that are an asset to any bed.

## SQUASHES **Summer and autumn**

Like chillies, squashes come in a fantastic range of different shapes and colours. Medium-sized varieties can be grown on wigwams, arches and obelisks to show off the fruits and improve ripening.

## WINTER SALAD LEAVES **Autumn, winter and spring** Hardy leaves like

rocket, lamb's lettuce and the most cold-tolerant endives and mustards can usually be harvested all winter, especially with the protection of a tunnel or cloche. With different leaf shapes, some tinged with red, they are a tempting sight in late winter – and just think of the vitamin C!

## Fruit

With beautiful blossom in spring and attractively ripening fruit in late summer, apples, pears, plums and other favourites compete with the best of ornamental garden trees. Trained espaliers or fans of these 'top fruit' have traditionally been used to enhance kitchen gardens. They make good screens or wall coverings, take up minimal space, and it's easy to pick the fruit. A warm wall is ideal for a peach, apricot, fig or pear (below, the pear variety 'Durondeau'), perhaps trained into a decorative fan shape, while a sunny arch or pergola could support a grape vine. In partial shade, grow soft fruit like raspberries and loganberries, while for fruit-growing on an altogether smaller scale, an attractive strawberry pot is hard to beat.

## Vintage accessories

The paraphernalia of a bygone age of kitchen gardening can be very appealing. Entire businesses now thrive on the trade in heritage gardening equipment, and reproductions are everywhere. Garden 'antiques' such as galvanized watering cans, forcing pots for seakale and rhubarb, or glazed hand-lights for bringing on early crops, are now marketed as desirable gifts at eye-watering prices. But it is still possible to pick up old tools, clay pots, buckets and other more utilitarian items quite cheaply, even though they are fast becoming collectables. Fashionable they may be, but they stood the test of time through the golden age of the kitchen garden and are often better designed, more durable and 'greener' than their mass-produced modern equivalents.

# The sensory garden

Every good garden is in fact a garden for all the senses. Smell generally comes a close second to sight in the way we experience and remember gardens and plants. Taste is up there too, of course, especially now that more and more people are discovering the joy and satisfaction of their own freshly grown food. The senses of touch and sound perhaps get less attention, but planning with all five senses in mind is a good route to a truly multi-dimensional garden.

## Sight

Designers, like architects, have a whole toolbox of subtle visual tricks and effects that they employ in order to achieve a particular atmosphere or mood (see page 87). These techniques depend on proportion, the use of light and shade, plant shapes, and – not least – the fact that different colours provoke different emotional and visual responses (see pages 83–7).

## Touch

If you've never given much thought to what plants are like to touch – leaves, flowers, fruit, stems and bark – you've been missing out on a whole range of experiences. Woolly or waxy, silky, spiny or fluffy are just some of the manifestations of this single aspect of the plant world. A sensory garden can explore and exploit all these and more, with visual contrasts as a welcome bonus. Try some of these easy, touchy-feely plants:

- *Ballota pseudodictamnus* Perennial shrub with felty leaves and bobbly flowerheads
- *Bergenia* Ground-cover perennial with leathery leaves
- *Carex buchananii* Perennial grass with wiry stems
- *Cotoneaster horizontalis* Winter-berrying shrub with a stiff, fishbone-like structure
- *Dipsacus fullonum* (teasel) Biennial with stiff, spiny stems and flowers
- *Helleborus* x *hybridus* Perennial with waxy winter flowers
- *Lunaria annua* (honesty) Biennial with crisp, papery seedpods
- *Pennisetum alopecuroides* Perennial grass with soft, fluffy 'bottlebrush' flowerheads
- *Polystichum setiferum* Fern with lacy fronds
- *Prunus serrula* Tree with smooth, satiny bark
- *Salvia argentea* Biennial with dramatic, woolly leaves
- *Stipa tenuissima* Perennial grass with soft, silky stems

## Taste

As a way of focusing attention on taste in the garden, try growing your own 'extreme taste' collection in decorative pots, just for fun, as a seasonal feature. It's a good way to get children involved in edible gardening, too. You and they

① Make the most of sensory plants by placing a seat where you can appreciate a range of them at close quarters. ② Include tactile grasses such as the fluffy *Pennisetum alopecuroides* 'Herbstzauber'.

will be astonished by the range of flavours you can produce in a small collection of easy-to-grow fruits, vegetables and herbs. Try some of the following (most of which can be grown from seed), and think up some more:

- Carrots (sweet, earthy)
- Cherry tomatoes (sweet)
- Chicory (bitter)
- Chillies (hot)
- Chives (oniony)
- Coriander (sweet-sour)
- Fennel (aniseed)
- Lemon verbena (citrus)
- Mint (tangy)
- Nasturtiums (peppery)
- Sorrel (sour, sharp)
- Strawberries (sweet)

## Sound

Birdsong and the sound of water are among our favourite garden sounds. But on a more down-to-earth level, your first thought on the subject may be how to protect your garden from the worst effects of unwelcome sounds: a noisy road, other people's music, barking dogs, domestic squabbles or power tools. Building a wall or landscaping a bank with dense planting on top are effective solutions, if rather drastic and almost certainly expensive. Plants alone can reduce outside noise considerably if carefully chosen, sited and grouped. A dense evergreen hedge or a group of shrubs will be the most effective.

Then there are plants that create their own gentle background music. Bamboo and miscanthus swish pleasantly in the slightest breeze for much of the year, while on warm, sunny days in late summer and autumn the dry seedpods of many plants produce a veritable symphony of

The sound of water in a garden should be subtle and gentle, as in Tom Stuart-Smith's water feature in the Laurent-Perrier garden at the Chelsea Flower Show in 2005.

popping and crackling. Certain trees, such as poplars and birch, have leaves that swoosh and hiss with the wind in summer. Everyone knows the sound of autumn leaves crunching underfoot, but the crisp leaves of hornbeam and beech hedges, which remain on the twigs, contribute a gentle clattering and rustling to the garden soundtrack all winter long.

## Smell

Fragrance is one of the most elusive of garden features, never really guaranteed (especially when you seek it out) but often taking you delightfully by surprise. Nothing is more satisfying than a truly fragrant garden – when it works. There are a range of plants to choose from in the box on the right, so start planting for scent in your garden all year round!

## Scents for all seasons

SPRING
*Azara microphylla* 'Variegata'
*Convallaria majalis* (lily-of-the-valley)
*Erysimum* (wallflower)
*Hyacinthus* (hyacinth)
*Lonicera periclymenum* 'Belgica' (honeysuckle)
*Narcissus poeticus* var. *recurvus*
*Osmanthus* x *burkwoodii*
*Syringa* (lilac)
*Viola odorata* (sweet violet)

SUMMER
*Aloysia triphylla* (lemon verbena)
*Buddleja davidii* (butterfly bush)
*Dianthus* (pinks and sweet williams)
*Heliotropium* (cherry pie)
*Jasminum officinale* (jasmine)
*Lathyrus odoratus* (sweet pea)
*Lavandula* (lavender)
*Lilium regale* (regal lily)
*Lonicera periclymenum* 'Serotina' (honeysuckle)
*Matthiola bicornis* (night-scented stock)
*Nicotiana sylvestris* (tobacco plant)
*Philadelphus* (mock orange)
*Rosa* (including 'Albertine', 'Gloire de Dijon' and many others)

AUTUMN
*Brugmansia*
*Clerodendrum trichotomum* var. *fargesii*
*Elaeagnus pungens*
*Juniperus communis* 'Hibernica'
*Mahonia japonica*
*Myrtus communis* (myrtle)
*Osmanthus heterophyllus* 'Variegatus'
*Pelargonium* (scented-leaved geranium)
*Viburnum farreri*
… and ripe fruit such as apples, plums …

WINTER
*Abeliophyllum distichum*
*Chimonanthus praecox* (winter sweet)
*Clematis armandii*
*Daphne bholua* 'Jacqueline Postill'
*Lonicera* x *purpusii* 'Winter Beauty'
*Mahonia* x *media* 'Winter Sun'
*Sarcococca confusa*
*Sarcococca hookeriana* var. *digyna*
*Viburnum* x *bodnantense* 'Dawn'

# The finishing touches

Though often an afterthought, garden furniture and accessories such as containers and garden sculpture should relate to the overall design just as indoor furniture is chosen to go with its setting. Seating areas tend to be focal points in a garden, whether planned that way or not, so choose furniture that you find pleasing to look at *and* to use.

## Garden furniture

Furniture that can be left out all year means no storage problems in winter. Permanent outdoor furniture also lets you take advantage of those impromptu (but so welcome and

memorable) sunny winter moments when it's warm enough to take your coffee outdoors. Most all-weather furniture is made from hardwood or non-corrosive metal such as aluminium. The range available

There's a whole world of garden furniture beyond the ordinary and mass-produced, and it's well worth looking around for something that's in just the right style for your garden – wheher it be chic, sleek, classic or rustic. Look for painted wire, rustic or sawn timber, stone (cold to sit on) or the relatively new all-weather rattan, which is weather-resistant and comfortable.

is huge, as are the prices quite often, but if you find something you really like it will be a worthwhile investment and, with care, can last a lifetime. With hardwood furniture, always check that it comes from environmentally responsible sources (*see* pages 57, 139).

For a traditional garden, where brand-new furniture can look starkly modern and incongruous, don't

Learn how to balance plants with their containers. Sometimes the plants will star, with the pot as a foil – or even completely hidden beneath the foliage. A really special pot or urn may not need plants at all.

dismiss the possibility of buying second-hand furniture. You might find just the right thing at an auction, in an antique or charity shop, or online. Well-built hardwood furniture in a classic style lasts for ages, acquiring a distinguished-looking silvery patina that looks perfect in a traditional garden.

## Containers

Containers suit every type of garden and are tremendously versatile. They can give a sense of balance and harmony if they reflect the planting elsewhere in the garden, or they can make a strong, definite focal point if they contrast with their surroundings. They have many practical purposes, too, brightening up patios and terraces where there is no soil, and enabling you to grow plants that may not like the soil in your garden. With the right care, pretty well any plant can be grown in a pot, at least for a short period.

## Container companions

An effective group of containers is a garden in itself, providing a welcome at the front door or an invitation to step out onto the patio. You can ring the changes with the seasons, or several times a season, without having to replant the whole thing as some plants fade, which you may need to do if mixing plants in a single container. Grouped pots retain moisture well, as they shelter each other from drying winds. Your display will work best if you choose containers of different sizes but similar in colour or style. For continuity and a feeling of harmony, try duplicating plants and containers, for example two or three pots of the same variety of tulip. Trailing plants look very elegant if they can cascade from a tall pot, or you can stand the container on bricks to give height – grouping other, smaller pots around it to disguise the base.

Decoratively moulded pots, or those with a pattern, look best when they contain plants with a strong shape and simple foliage, such as a plain-leaved cordyline or a clipped box. Conversely, intricate plants such as a mixture of houseleeks are better suited to a plain container.

The growing trend for using our gardens as outdoor rooms in summer has given them a new lease of life after dark. Patios, furniture, barbecues, lighting and all the paraphernalia of outdoor living are now found in most gardens and are much used for evening meals and entertaining. It's worth giving just as much attention to the garden setting and planting, creating the best possible backdrop for those memorable, balmy evenings when it seems that summer will never end.

### Colour and light levels

Planting for evening effect is not normally a top priority, but certain colours make such a dramatic difference to a garden at dusk and after dark that it's worth choosing a few plants with this in mind. The impact of various colours changes spectacularly towards the end of the day. Low, late afternoon sunshine emphasizes reds and oranges, but these colours then recede and have all but disappeared by dusk. Blues then take their place as the dominant colours after sunset and, as darkness approaches, it is the whites that occupy centre stage, taking on a new, luminous character and reflecting every scrap of dim light so the garden appears ghostly and atmospheric. White-variegated leaves and white stems create a similar effect, so you will have no shortage of plants from which to choose (*see* box, right, for some ideas).

Fragrance, too, is an integral part of the pleasure of strolling or sitting in the garden on summer evenings (*see* page 111). Fortunately, many white flowers – those of jasmine, *Nicotiana sylvestris*,

Choose lighting for the style of your garden: ① spotlights suit contemporary architectural planting; ② these slender lanterns hold their own in a more traditional setting.
Planting for evening: ③ a grass walk disappears into the shadows, with blue highlights for dusk; ④ a mixed border has phlox and evening primrose for after-hours fragrance.

*Lilium regale*, philadelphus and many roses – are also swooningly fragrant, so these plants earn their keep twice over.

**Garden lighting**

The sophisticated hardware that sometimes seems to be taking over our lives and our gardens now includes a vast range of outdoor lighting, both for safety and security, and for atmospheric effect. Subtle, gentle lighting is best to preserve the ambience and the sense of mystery of a garden in the gloaming. Once your eyes have adjusted to the lower light levels, you'll be able to see much more than you thought. Bright outdoor lights of any sort make it difficult to see the stars, give unpleasantly harsh contrasts and deep shadows, and can annoy your neighbours. Take care not to cause unnecessary light pollution, especially in country areas, and use downward-pointing lights wherever possible. If you do decide to use an uplighter, for example to highlight a tree or architectural plant – which, admittedly, can look wonderful – then be sure to leave the lights on only while you're actually using them.

The most successful lighting is conceived as part of the garden's overall design, and is best installed with the rest of the hard landscaping to save disruption later. It's advisable to use a qualified electrician to install any outdoor electrics. Modern low-voltage systems are much safer than their predecessors, but they need mains connections that are safe and that comply with up-to-date regulations.

For those who prefer their nights dark and don't want to go in for garden lighting in a big way, the wide range and easy availability of solar-

powered lights and economical, energy-efficient LEDs now makes it easy and cheap to install unobtrusive lighting in places where you need it for safety or convenience, such as on steps and along paths.

## White plants for summer evenings

*Betula utilis* var. *jacquemontii*
*Clematis* 'Marie Boisselot'
*Cornus alternifolia* 'Argentea'
*Crambe cordifolia*
*Digitalis purpurea* f. *albiflora*
*Eryngium giganteum* 'Silver Ghost'
*Euonymus fortunei* 'Silver Queen'
*Euphorbia characias* 'Silver Swan'
*Fuchsia magellanica* var. *molinae*
*Gypsophila paniculata*
*Hydrangea anomala* subsp. *petiolaris*
*Iris pallida* 'Variegata'
*Jasminum officinale*
*Leucanthemum vulgare*
*Lilium regale*
*Mentha suaveolens* 'Variegata'
*Onopordum acanthium*
*Philadelphus coronarius* 'Variegatus' (below)
*Rosa* 'Félicité Perpétue'
*Rosa* 'Madame Alfred Carrière'

## Wildlife at night

On a warm, quiet evening, it's a privilege to share the after-hours world of the creatures that live in and around your garden. Many of the most tuneful birds, such as blackbirds and song thrushes, sing long after sunset, and are easier to hear once the hubbub of the day has died down. If you are lucky you may hear the haunting calls of owls, typically the familiar 'tu-whit, tu-whoo' of a pair of tawny owls, or the unearthly shriek of a barn owl. Look out for bats hunting for insects, silhouetted against the darkening sky on still, damp evenings. And when you are planning your planting, make provision for the fascinating array of night-flying moths that may visit honeysuckle (below top), evening primroses, stocks, red valerian, *Verbena bonariensis* (below bottom) and many other nectar-bearing plants.

# Season by season

Our changing climate means that autumn is lasting longer and spring beginning earlier, with the period in between shrinking correspondingly. Cutting the grass in midwinter – unheard of, not so long ago – is now quite commonplace, and more people than ever before are gardening all year round. So, the design challenge is to make our gardens look interesting throughout the year, so that seasonal highlights follow on from each other thick and fast, with no dull gaps in between.

# Planning for all-year interest

Yes, your garden can look attractive and give pleasure for 365 days a year. Making this a reality means using a wide variety of plants, and combining them for seasonal succession in a way that makes the most of every inch of available space.

## Where to begin?

We tend to associate certain plant effects with certain times of year: bulbs and blossom for spring, leaf colour and berries for autumn, evergreens for winter. Planning a succession of effects like this is a good starting point for an all-season garden. Begin to think of your favourite plants not in isolation, but as members of a cast of characters each contributing in its own season.

## Doubling up on space

But how do you fit all these different plants in – especially if you have a small garden? The surprising thing is how little space even some of the most valuable players need. Spring bulbs, for example, can be tucked in under deciduous shrubs, or close to the crowns of perennials that follow the bulbs, or at the back of a bed. A spring-blossoming tree or shrub might support a summer-flowering climber, adding dramatically to the

overall impact without gobbling up your precious ground space.

## Multi-tasking

Some of the stars in your cast will perform more than once in the year. Some may flower for a second time if cut back after their first flowering, such as anthemis, lupins and some roses. Even more usefully, some plants play different roles at different times – an ornamental hawthorn with spring blossom, colourful autumn foliage and winter berries, or a sedum or phlomis with good foliage, summer flowers and winter seedheads. It's all about getting the maximum effect, from the minimum space, for the longest time.

Planting for a succession of effects: silky *Stipa tenuissima*, attractive all year, partners the summer flowers of eryngiums and alliums, which will turn into shapely autumn seedheads.

Strongly positioned evergreens and a broad mix of different plant types are guiding principles in this successful all-season garden, seen here in early autumn.

# Spring

Everyone can have a garden that looks good in spring. After a run of winter days when nothing seems to change much in the garden, it's such a relief when everything begins to turn green that you almost find yourself welcoming the weeds with open arms. But in this season when gardening seems so easy, there's lots of scope for planning and planting to make your garden even better, now and for the rest of the year.

## Spring colours

There is so much green around in spring that all colours seem harmonious, even the clashing combinations that might jar the nerves at other times of year when they are less likely to be diluted by lashings of greenery. It's tempting to take a completely laissez-faire attitude to colour in spring, when seemingly anything goes and we're grateful for all of it. But there are some uniquely springlike colour combinations that are worth setting up deliberately because they seem to capture the essence of this freshest and purest of seasons. Blue, white, yellow and green dominate the early months of the year in the countryside, when woodland,

*Malus transitoria,* an unusual crab-apple – a beautiful tree in spring, and again in autumn when it bears tiny golden fruits.

especially, is at its best. These same colours echoed in your garden will look brilliant, too.

## Woodland plants

The appeal of woodland in spring lies in the classic wildflowers that thrive there – bluebells, primroses and wood anemones in particular. These plants are perfectly adapted to life beneath deciduous trees, flowering while they get plenty of light – before the trees come into leaf – then enjoying the cool shade of the tree canopy for the rest of the year. You can replicate this very successfully in the garden. Try it under trees – where a tapestry of ground-covering woodlanders and spring bulbs may be better than grass, which struggles to cope

A wonderfully fresh mix of early-season colour with hellebores, erythroniums, primulas and euphorbias – woodlanders that will enjoy tree cover later in the year.

with summer shade – or beneath deciduous shrubs whose moment of glory comes later and will mask anything at ground level that is looking past its best.

## Design tips and tasks for spring

Plan your spring displays with the possibility of late frosts in mind; despite climate change, they can still take you by surprise and do a lot of damage. Soft young leaves, and early spring flowers such as camellias and magnolias, are especially vulnerable if the early morning sun falls on frosted plants, so avoid an east-facing position for those that will be susceptible. The emerging shoots of lilies can be protected by planting them among low shrubs – these will provide some cover as the lilies start into growth.

Make a new year's resolution to try at least one plant that you've never grown before. For best results and a better long-term investment, plan what it will be, exactly where you will plant it and how it will enhance your garden, before you go to the garden centre and part with your hard-earned cash.

As always, think what's coming next. Consider how to prevent plants that are going over from spoiling the show. Dying daffodil leaves are easy to hide in longer grass or at the back of a border, but the foliage of alliums becomes unsightly and yellow even while they are flowering in late spring. You can hide it successfully by planting alliums with low shrubs that are complementary in form or colour, such as *Salvia officinalis*

## Don't go with the flow!

Spring gardens everywhere abound with daffodils, forsythia and pink cherry blossom, but there are so many other good spring plants that are readily available and make a welcome change. Dare to be different, and plant a few unusual things that you won't see everywhere else.

**TREES**
*Amelanchier lamarckii*
*Cercis siliquastrum*
*Malus transitoria*

**SHRUBS**
*Cornus mas* 'Variegata' (below)
*Ribes speciosum*
*Viburnum carlesii* 'Aurora'

**PERENNIALS**
*Euphorbia myrsinites*
*Pulsatilla vulgaris*
*Saxifraga x urbium*

**BULBS**
*Muscari botryoides* 'Album'
*Scilla bifolia*
*Tulipa linifolia*

'Purpurascens' (purple sage). Grow other bulbs with perennials such as *Geranium psilostemon* or *Astrantia*, whose foliage will soon billow up and cover everything beneath.

Rig up support for herbaceous plants, such as delphiniums, that will need it, well before they are in danger of flopping over. Proprietary plant supports in dark colours are an option, but twigs and natural jute twine, or twiggy prunings, are surprisingly effective, subtle and (even better) biodegradable.

## Easy plant groupings for a woodland effect

*Brunnera macrophylla* 'Jack Frost' (blue and silver)
*Convallaria majalis* (lily-of-the-valley) (white)
*Narcissus* 'Jenny' (creamy white)
*Pulmonaria* 'Lewis Palmer' (deep-blue flower, white-spotted foliage)
*Veronica umbrosa* 'Georgia Blue'

*Hyacinthus orientalis* 'Blue Jacket' (deep blue)
*Leucojum aestivum* (white and green)
*Lamium maculatum* 'White Nancy' (white and green)
*Narcissus* 'Jack Snipe' (creamy white and yellow)
*Primula vulgaris* (primrose) (pale yellow)

*Ajuga reptans* 'Catlin's Giant' (lavender blue)
*Anemone blanda* (lavender blue)
*Euphorbia amygdaloides* var. *robbiae* (acid yellow-green)
*Origanum vulgare* 'Aureum' (gold)
*Viola riviniana* Purpurea Group (purple flower, bronze foliage)

Save on summer watering by mulching flower beds in early spring, while the soil is still damp. This will also help to keep the weeds at bay.

# Summer

Ah, at last it's here – that profusion of flowers, and fragrance, and balmy days that we dream about all year. It's so important to relax and enjoy the garden now – otherwise what's the point of all the work? But from a design and planning point of view, summer is quite a challenge. It's hard to keep on top of everything when it's all growing so fast, and only careful forethought will prevent that dispiriting change from everything in the garden being lovely to everything being past it.

*Echinacea purpurea* is a great plant for late summer, provided your soil isn't too dry. Its distinctive shape and unusual colouring make it a good partner for many other flowers, and it's good to pick for the house too.

## Summer – early and late

When you're working out a planting scheme, somehow early summer seems to take care of itself. So many of the indispensable chocolate-box stars belong to this time of year: roses, pinks, clematis, irises, and staple flowering shrubs like philadelphus and deutzia. No

worries there, then. But late summer is a different matter, and a little advance planning is definitely required to stop mixed planting from going into a slow, premature decline. Bedding plants have long been the traditional tool to keep the show going, but if you don't want the bother of bedding out, there is a select band of 'must-have' shrubs and perennials that can be relied on to keep flowering right on into autumn (*see* box, left).

## Exotic planting

Balmy summer days lend themselves to exotic planting, which has become fashionable in recent years – as it was in Victorian times. There's a great thrill to be had in transforming a suburban garden into a tropical oasis bursting with luxuriant vegetation and smouldering colour; and excitement, too, in the sheer speed with which some tender plants grow in warm weather.

If you have a conservatory or heated greenhouse to keep them warm over winter, you can grow true exotic perennials such as bougainvillea and *Brugmansia* (formerly *Datura*), agaves, cacti and succulents like echeverias and aeoniums. These are tender plants that would be unlikely to stand British winters outdoors. But even without winter heat, you can use a sheltered, warm area of the garden to plant a permanent framework of hardy plants that have exotic-looking foliage or flowers (*see* box right). In summer, these become a backdrop for colourful dahlias, begonias, cannas and salvias (which can be overwintered as dry tubers), and tender annuals grown from seed – perhaps tithonias, ipomoeas,

### Late-summer stalwarts

*Anemone hupehensis* 'Hadspen Abundance'

*Aster* x *frikartii* 'Mönch'

*Caryopteris* × *clandonensis* 'Heavenly Blue'

*Ceratostigma willmottianum*

*Dahlia* 'Bishop of Llandaff'

*Echinacea purpurea*

*Eupatorium maculatum* Atropurpureum Group

*Fuchsia* 'Riccartonii'

*Hyssopus officinalis*

*Penstemon* 'Andenken an Friedrich Hahn'

*Perovskia atriplicifolia* 'Blue Spire'

*Sedum* 'Herbstfreude'

The late Christopher Lloyd's legendary exotic garden at Great Dixter. Plants shown here include banana plants, dahlias, castor-oil plant and the tender purple grass *Pennisetum setaceum* 'Rubrum'. Not a low-maintenance option, but an exciting one.

## Hardy 'exotics'

*Catalpa bignonioides* (coppice in winter for vigorous growth and big leaves)

*Cordyline australis*

*Cotinus* 'Grace' (pollard in winter for the best foliage)

*Crocosmia* 'Lucifer'

*Eucalyptus gunnii*

*Fatsia japonica*

*Kniphofia*

*Musa basjoo* (the hardiest banana plant, but still best covered in winter)

*Paulownia tomentosa* (coppice in winter to get huge leaves)

*Phormium cookianum* subsp.*hookeri* 'Cream Delight'

*Verbena bonariensis*

*Vitis vinifera* 'Purpurea'

*Yucca filamentosa* 'Bright Edge'

zinnias, cosmos, ornamental gourds and the poisonous but eye-catching foliage plant *Ricinus communis*.

## Design tips and tasks for summer

Take lots of photographs of your beds and borders through the summer to help you plan improvements for next year. Note conspicuous gaps, colour combinations (those you don't like as well as those you do) and plants that are getting too big for their boots and suffocating their neighbours. Digital photography has such a useful role to play in garden design, enabling you to collect photographs – easily and inexpensively – of areas of your garden. Combinations that worked well can be repeated, and you can set aside photos of less successful plantings for when you have more time in the winter. Then either print these out and draw on them, or even try manipulating them digitally, to try out improvements.

Spend just a few minutes dead-heading, as often as you can, to keep the show going. This will pay dividends with bedding plants and annuals, especially, but many perennials will be coaxed into a second and third flowering, too. With roses, take off not just the dead flowerhead, which will leave an ugly stump, but also the stem below it – back to a promising-looking bud.

While you are dead-heading, look out for pests and diseases, so you can deal with them before they become a serious problem. Particular troublemakers include the unmistakable red lily beetle, most active on sunny days, and, of course, slugs and snails on wet nights.

Keep a few 'special' plants like agapanthus and lilies in large pots, and use them as temporary fillers when a gap appears in your borders, or as focal points on the patio or beside the front door.

Don't neglect topiary. Smartly clipped, it works wonders with a border that has become a bit too luxuriant and overblown and needs rescuing. Compact box balls, yew cones or dwarf junipers, either in elegant pots or planted in the ground at a border's edge, lend a formal touch that makes the planting picture look intentionally romantic and 'cottagey' – rather than just unkempt.

### Don't forget

Keep a design eye open and note, for example, whether you have the right balance of sun and shade in different areas of the garden, so that you can do something about it in the winter.

# Autumn

Late summer often brings a bit of a lull in the garden. What with holidays, and in some years the lethargy induced by hot weather, things tend to cruise along, and planting and weeding take a back seat. With the start of autumn come cooler nights, rain perhaps, and a change of gear as spring bulbs go on sale and planning for next year comes into focus. But there are lots of plants to enjoy in autumn, too.

Autumn shapes and colours at Marchants Hardy Plants in Sussex. Globe artichoke flowers and dark agapanthus rise above soft clouds of santolina, perovskia and diascia.

## Autumn specials

Our changing climate is making a big difference to autumn, gradually transforming it from the beginning of the end of the gardening year into a season in its own right. Low sunshine, and the feeling of wanting to have a 'last fling' before winter, turn autumn into a wonderful opportunity to make the most of really dazzling colour in the garden – not just traditional leaf colour but the bold, oil-paint hues of late flowers. The first frost comes later, so the tender, 'firecracker' plants – such as zinnias, salvias, dahlias and fuchsias – carry on flowering for many weeks, going from strength to strength if the weather is kind. Hardy, late-flowering shrubs also have a longer season of colour, so abelias, hibiscus and some hebes, as well as *Caryopteris* x *clandonensis*, *Ceratostigma willmottianum* and *Perovskia atriplicifolia*, are all much more likely to make a long-lasting contribution to the garden. Then there are grasses, seen at their best when low, golden sunshine highlights the unique structure of each variety. Miscanthus and pennisetum, in their many cultivated forms, are among the old faithfuls that look really outstanding in autumn, but try something less well known too – perhaps the unusually shaped *Chasmanthium latifolium*.

## Ornamental trees

Everyone loves autumn colour, and certain trees are frequently recommended specifically for this purpose. But to earn its space in a garden, a tree needs to do more than one thing. Choose those that have a starring role in autumn but give a good supporting performance in other seasons too.

■ *Acer capillipes* (snake-bark maple) Green and grey stripy bark gives all-year interest. The leaves are a good shape too, bright red in bud in spring, and russet in autumn.

■ *Amelanchier lamarckii* (snowy mespilus) With delicate, white, starry flowers among bronze leaves, amelanchiers are among the prettiest small trees for spring

Autumn sunshine and *Stipa gigantea* might have been made for each other. This wonderful grass needs an uncluttered setting, and looks even better against a dark background.

*Amelanchier lamarckii* deserves to be more widely planted as a garden tree. Its attractive foliage partners delicate blossom in spring, and finally builds to a fiery autumn show.

blossom. Autumn colour is striking, too, and in late summer the fruits ripen, attracting hungry birds.

■ *Crataegus persimilis* 'Prunifolia' This is a good, tough, all-round

ornamental hawthorn, with a froth of creamy May blossom. The autumn leaves turn very gradually from green to yellow to a warm scarlet, and there are plenty of long-lasting red berries that blackbirds will relish in hard winter weather.

■ *Malus* (crab apple) The spring blossom of the various crabs develops into a range of different, colourful autumn fruits. Those of *Malus* 'John Downie' are large, oval and orange-red (great for crab-apple jelly), while those of *Malus* x *zumi* 'Golden Hornet' are like tiny, deep-yellow apples.

■ *Mespilus germanica* (medlar) This medium-sized, rounded tree has attractive pinkish-white spring blossom, golden leaves in autumn, and curious brown fruits on its bare winter branches.

## Design tips and tasks for autumn

Fend off those end-of-summer lows by spending a wet early autumn afternoon with a bulb catalogue, planning a dazzling show to last from late winter to late spring. Before you order, think (and note down) where you will plant each sort of bulb so that you know exactly what you're doing when the bulbs arrive. Try out a few bulbs you haven't grown before, and don't forget the 'tinies' – small, early-flowering treasures like scillas and chionodoxas that can be tucked in almost anywhere, building up colonies over the years to make a real impact.

Plant or move hardy shrubs and perennials in autumn, when there are several months of winter rain

The abundant yellow crab-apples of *Malus* x *zumi* 'Golden Hornet' will brighten the dullest autumn days.

ahead to bed them in. Climate change is tending to bring milder, wetter winters and an increased risk of spring drought, so planting now is a better bet than leaving it until spring. Order bare-rooted trees, plus fruit and hedging, ready for planting from November, when they start to become dormant.

Make a stylish display of attractive containers for a porch or patio to last through the winter. Plant them up with ivies, small evergreens with good foliage, berrying shrubs and sedges – anything that looks appealing at your garden centre or nursery. When they have made decent-sized specimens in a year or so, plant them out in the garden.

### Don't forget

Collect seed from faded annuals, biennials and perennials that you hope will self-sow, in case they don't make their own arrangements.

# Winter

There's more happening in the winter garden than we are inclined to think, and not all of it is going on underground. Preparations for the new season are, naturally, going on down there as bulbs start into growth and promising new shoots get ready to emerge. Evergreens, bare stems and colourful bark, shrubs with fragrant flowers, and the intricate skeletons left by flowering perennials all add up to a subtly attractive scene, and there is time to appreciate each one so much more during this quiet season.

Teasels are a winter essential – beautiful when coated in frost, thrilling when visited by goldfinches.

## Architectural seedheads

There is a select group of plants – mainly annuals and biennials – that make a great contribution to the garden in autumn and winter with their decorative seedheads. These are some of the best:

■ *Dipsacus fullonum* (teasel) This is a fine architectural biennial, though you must weed out unwanted seedlings while they are still small – a combination of prickles and a tenacious tap root makes it difficult later. The seedheads provide winter structure and look striking in frost and snow, as well as attracting that most beautiful of birds, the goldfinch, to feast on their nourishing seeds.

■ *Eryngium giganteum* Another thistly biennial, this has shapely, silvery bracts that give it great presence, and earn it a place in a mixed border where it will probably self-seed. It may take two or three years to flower, and its seedheads are not long-lasting, but in a dry season some of them may last well into autumn.

■ *Lunaria annua* (honesty) Cottage gardens are not complete without honesty, whose translucent 'pennies' gleam in winter sunshine. It is beautiful in dried arrangements, too, especially if you are patient enough to peel off the outer casing of each shiny seedpod. (Save the seeds for next year!)

■ *Nicandra physalodes* (shoo-fly plant) This unusual, fast-growing annual, not unlike a Chinese lantern, has pretty china-blue flowers that become shapely 'lanterns' of a moody purple-black, and hang in neat rows. The coarse foliage will droop and decay with the first frost.

■ *Nigella damascena* (love-in-a-mist) The delicate, papery seedpods of this much-loved cottage annual develop from (usually) blue flowers. It's useful for knitting a border together, and light enough in stature never to get in the way.

■ *Papaver somniferum* (opium poppy) The globular, 'salt-shaker' seedheads of these poppies make a distinctive feature, and they can last well into winter.

■ *Phlomis russeliana* This robust perennial has felty, heart-shaped leaves and stiff tiers of yellow flowers. The symmetrical seedheads that follow and persist through winter outlast many others in the garden.

■ *Sedum* 'Herbstfreude' This trusty sedum is an asset to the garden from late spring, when its broccoli-like flowerheads begin to appear, right through to late winter, when you'll probably feel you must finally cut the russet seedheads down.

## Design tips and tasks for winter

Plant for Christmas – even a small garden has room for a clipped, berrying holly in a pot, which you could stand beside the front door as a seasonal welcome. Try *Ilex aquifolium* 'J.C. van Tol', which fruits reasonably reliably without a partner (in order to fruit, most hollies need a non-berrying male plant within range of the berrying female). Grow and pick some fragrant evergreen foliage for making a wreath to hang on the front door and for decorating inside: myrtle, cypress, rosemary and bay are all good choices.

For your first gardening task of the new year, cut the old foliage off your hellebores. The new season's flowers will show up much better, and any disfiguring fungal disease is less likely to be transferred from the old foliage to the new.

Appreciate your winter plants at close quarters by picking regular offerings for the house, and by planting some late winter bulbs such as snowdrops and early scillas in small pots to enjoy indoors. You can plant them outside, wherever there is a gap, after they've flowered.

### Don't forget

Fine, frost-free dry days are ideal for any hard landscaping work that needs doing, from building raised beds (*see* page 43) to laying paths (*see* pages 58–9).

### Distinctive bark and stems

**TREES**
*Acer griseum*
*Arbutus unedo*
*Betula utilis* var. *jacquemontii*
*Prunus serrula*

**SHRUBS**
*Cornus alba* 'Elegantissima'
*Cornus sanguinea* 'Midwinter Fire'
*Cornus sericea* 'Flaviramea'
*Rubus thibetanus*
*Salix alba* var. *vitellina* 'Britzensis' (below)
*Salix daphnoides* 'Aglaia'

The Christmas rose (*Helleborus niger*) can be quite tricky to please but is a joy where it succeeds.

### 'Winter sunshine' plants

There's nothing like gold in the garden to bring 'sunshine' to a drab winter day. There are plenty of evergreens whose leaves will do the trick, but also golden flowers, berries and stems. Try these:

*Aucuba japonica* 'Crotonifolia' (large evergreen shrub, yellow-splashed leaves)

*Choisya ternata* 'Sundance' (medium evergreen shrub, yellow leaves)

*Cornus sericea* 'Flaviramea' (large deciduous shrub, greenish-gold stems)

*Elaeagnus pungens* 'Maculata' (large evergreen shrub, yellow-splashed leaves)

*Eranthis hyemalis* (dwarf yellow-flowered bulb)

*Euonymus fortunei* 'Emerald 'n' Gold' (dwarf evergreen shrub, yellow-variegated leaves)

*Hedera helix* 'Buttercup' (evergreen climber, yellow leaves)

*Hedera helix* 'Goldheart' (evergreen climber, yellow-variegated leaves)

*Ilex* x *altaclerensis* 'Golden King' (large evergreen shrub, yellow-variegated leaves)

*Jasminum nudiflorum* (medium deciduous shrub, yellow flowers) (below)

*Mahonia* x *media* 'Winter Sun' (medium evergreen shrub, yellow flowers)

*Malus transitoria* (deciduous tree, golden fruits)

*Osmanthus heterophyllus* 'Goshiki' (medium evergreen shrub, yellow-splashed leaves)

*Pyracantha* 'Saphyr Jaune' (large, thorny wall shrub, golden berries)

*Sorbus* 'Joseph Rock' (deciduous tree, golden berries)

# Planting solutions

'No problems, only solutions,' goes the optimistic saying. But talk to anyone who is battling to establish a garden on a waterlogged or gale-torn site and they could be forgiven for thinking the opposite. The important thing to remember if you have a difficult garden is that it's always much easier and less costly to adapt the garden and planting to the site rather than the other way round. There are very few places where literally nothing will grow – it's just a question of finding plants that will tolerate and even enjoy your conditions. Adopt a flexible approach and the solution will present itself.

# Problem gardens

There are always practical challenges to be met when you're making or maintaining a garden. Poor soil, pests and diseases, and the wrong sort of weather are common grumbles, but we gardeners derive great satisfaction from outwitting the gremlins and succeeding against all the odds.

Not just for Christmas – hollies (here, *Ilex aquifolium* 'J.C. van Tol') may grow quite slowly when young but, once established, they are reliable stalwarts for year-round interest on all sorts of difficult sites.

At one time, specific types of 'problem' plot would have discouraged even the most intrepid gardener, bent on creating the one-size-fits-all, conventional garden (lawn, bedding plants, roses, shrubbery) that used to be the template for every suburban plot. But today's gardens are far more individual and, with a little imagination, creative solutions and the right planting can transform even the most unpromising site.

Improving the soil is fundamental to meeting almost every kind of garden challenge. Adding organic matter, in the form of compost, well-rotted manure or a proprietary soil conditioner, will add moisture-retaining body to dry soils, and nutrients and air to wet ones. It will nourish starved ground in the shade cast by trees, especially evergreens, and encourage plants to make the large, healthy root systems that they need for stability in windy gardens.

Aided by regular cultivation and the removal of weeds, a sterile building site will gradually transform itself into a fertile garden.

## Survivors

Each kind of problem garden will have its own plant solutions, but there are some naturally tough and robust plants that seem able to cope better than most. So don't despair before you've tried growing some of the following:

## Trees

*Acer campestre*; *Betula pendula*; *Carpinus betulus*; *Crataegus* x *lavalleei* 'Carrierei'; *Ilex aquifolium*; *Sorbus aria* 'Lutescens'; *Sorbus hupehensis*

## Shrubs

*Buxus sempervirens* 'Elegantissima'; *Cornus alba* 'Elegantissima'; *Cotoneaster simonsii*; *Euonymus fortunei* 'Emerald Gaiety'; *Hebe pinguifolia* 'Pagei'; *Ilex aquifolium* 'Handsworth New Silver'; *Jasminum nudiflorum*; *Lonicera pileata*; *Lonicera* × *purpusii* 'Winter Beauty'; *Osmanthus* × *burkwoodii*; *Osmanthus heterophyllus* 'Variegatus'; *Phlomis fruticosa*; *Potentilla fruticosa* cultivars; *Prunus lusitanica*; *Rosa* 'Fru Dagmar Hastrup'; *Rosa glauca*; *Rosmarinus officinalis*; *Sambucus nigra* cultivars; *Sarcococca confusa*; *Viburnum opulus* 'Compactum'

## Climbers

*Clematis* 'Comtesse de Bouchaud'; *Clematis* 'Etoile Violette'; *Clematis tangutica*; × *Fatshedera lizei*; *Hedera helix* 'Duckfoot' ; *Hedera helix* 'Parsley Crested'; *Humulus lupulus* 'Aureus'; *Lathyrus latifolius*; *Lonicera periclymenum* 'Graham Thomas'; *Rosa* 'Compassion'; *Solanum crispum* 'Glasnevin'; *Vitis coignetiae*

## Herbaceous plants

*Anthemis tinctoria* 'E.C. Buxton'; *Campanula poscharskyana* 'Stella'; *Centaurea montana*; *Centranthus ruber*; *Digitalis purpurea*; *Doronicum orientale*; *Erigeron karvinskianus*; *Eryngium giganteum*; *Euphorbia amygdaloides* var. *robbiae*; *Geranium macrorrhizum* 'Album'; *Geranium* × *magnificum*; *Iris sibirica* 'Tropic Night'; *Papaver orientale*; *Sisyrinchium striatum*; *Stachys byzantina*; *Veronica umbrosa* 'Georgia Blue'; *Viola riviniana* Purpurea Group (*See also* box, page 95.)

## Bulbs

*Allium hollandicum*, *Chionodoxa luciliae*; *Crocus tommasinianus*; *Cyclamen hederifolium*; *Leucojum aestivum*; *Narcissus* 'Jack Snipe'; *Nectaroscordum siculum*; *Scilla siberica*; *Tulipa* 'Ballerina'

## Grasses

*Carex buchananii*; *Carex oshimensis* 'Evergold'; *Luzula sylvatica* 'Marginata'; *Miscanthus sinensis* 'Morning Light'; *Stipa tenuissima*

# New-build gardens

If you buy a newly built house, the chances of its coming complete with a thoughtfully landscaped garden topped with a foot or two of fertile loam are, frankly, not great. Clay subsoil on the surface may well have been hidden under poor-quality turf, and all manner of horrors, from brick rubble and waste mortar to cement bags, may lurk beneath. How, then, do you make this buried building site into a garden you can enjoy?

On a brand new plot you have a big advantage in that you can broadly plan the garden at the outset and have any earth-moving done while machinery is on site and access easy – a big cost saving. If you find it hard to envisage your new garden, arm yourself with the site plan and sketch a layout on paper.

## Container solutions

It can be prohibitively expensive to stock an entire new garden with plants big enough to make an impact within the first year or two – specimen-sized shrubs in 10- or 20-litre pots don't come cheap. But, if you aren't ready to plant the whole garden in the first season, you can still gain time by buying some of the shrubs you want and using them as container plants in a patio display for the first couple of years. They'll soon catch up with those pricey, more mature plants. Choose reliable garden-centre plants in 2- or 3-litre pots and re-pot them into bigger containers full of rich compost, with a dash of slow-release fertilizer. Either use normal 10-litre plastic pots and put them inside a more attractive container, or plant them into an ornamental pot (avoid narrow necks – they make it hard to get the rootball out later).

### Traditional terracing

If your new-build, empty garden is on a steep slope, now's the time to turn this to advantage by terracing. This way of making slopes into flat, usable ground stretches back to prehistoric times. It is just as valid on modern building plots as on ancient cultivation terraces. Each level needs to be retained, usually by a brick or blockwork wall. It's often nice to have them at 'perching height' – about 60cm (2ft) – as additional seating. If there's enough lateral space on a steep slope, then two terraces of that height will look better and provide more stability than a single retaining wall of twice the height. For walls that will stand higher than a metre (40in), consult a structural engineer about design and building.

### Space-fillers for quick impact

*Cosmos bipinnatus* (annual)
*Fuchsia magellanica*
*Humulus lupulus* 'Aureus'
*Lupinus arboreus* (below)
*Onopordum acanthium*
*Tropaeolum majus* (nasturtium – annual)

A few well-sited container plants will soften newly built steps and retaining walls until the permanent planting matures enough to take over.

## KEY to symbols

In this chapter the following symbols are used to indicate a plant's preferred growing conditions. All plants featured are fully hardy. A rough idea is also given as to what height (H) and spread (S) might be at maturity.

- ○ Prefers/tolerates an open, sunny site
- ◐ Prefers/tolerates some shade
- ● Prefers/tolerates full shade
- ◗ Needs wet soil
- ◗ Needs moist soil
- ◇ Needs dry soil
- ⇊ Needs well-drained soil
- pH↓ Needs/prefers acidic soil
- pH↑ Needs/prefers alkaline soil
- ◖ Needs humus-rich soil
- ❖ Season of main interest (e.g. flowers, foliage, stems, berries)

# Plants for quick impact in new-build gardens

## Allium cristophii

○ ◊ ⚎ ❖SUMMER

H 50cm (20in) S 20cm (8in)

The larger alliums are real 'statement' plants, strongly architectural and giving instant impact to a garden. Their flowering season is short, but *Allium cristophii* makes up for it with its wonderful long-lasting seedheads. Plant alliums with low shrubs and perennials that will hide their dying leaves.

## Buddleja 'Lochinch'

○ ◊ ⚎ ❖ SUMMER

H 2.5m (8ft) S 3m (10ft)

Vigorous and long-suffering even in the most unpromising situations, buddleias will make good cover in no time in a new garden and, as everyone knows, butterflies love them. Some varieties, though, have straggly foliage and a gawky, gaunt habit, which means they don't contribute much when they aren't in flower. 'Lochinch' is a hybrid with soft grey foliage and quite pale lavender flowers. Prune it hard every spring to keep it shapely and flowering well.

## Ceanothus 'Concha'

○ ⚎ ❖SPRING

H 2.5m (8ft) S 2.5m (8ft)

This fast-growing evergreen shrub is ideal for covering sunny walls and fences quickly, usually reaching a height of 2m (6ft) in its second season. It is covered in beautiful deep-blue blossom in late spring, and is a good host plant for a climber, such as a clematis, that will flower later. It's important to trim the plant back after flowering to stop it from bulging forwards. If that happens, the base will be shaded and lose its leaves – and ceanothus cannot be pruned back into old wood.

## Lavatera × clementii 'Barnsley'

○ ◊ ⚎ ❖ SUMMER

H 1.5m (5ft) S 1.2m (4ft)

This is probably the best known of several cultivars of the tree mallow (formerly *Lavatera olbia*) – all of them fast-growing, rather leggy shrubs. They have pink flowers over a long season, ranging from the pale pink 'Barnsley' to the purplish 'Burgundy Wine'. They are not long-lived, but their rapid growth makes them useful for quick colour, especially on dry soil. The plants are best bought small; larger specimens in pots can be top-heavy.

## Nigella damascena
Love-in-a-mist

○ ⚎ ❖SUMMER

H 50cm (20in) S 30cm (12in)

A favourite annual, with feathery foliage and shapely seedheads, Nigella is very forgiving of poor soil and self-seeds freely and conveniently. It lends a 'cottagey' effect to the garden and never becomes a nuisance. Blue is the principal (and by far the best) colour, but it is also available in white and pink, and is good for cut flowers.

## Rosa glauca

○ ⚎ ❖SUMMER TO WINTER

H 2.5m (8ft) S 1.5m (5ft)

This easily grown species rose is an unassuming but valuable background plant, offering attractive pinkish-grey foliage with clear cerise-pink, single flowers in early summer. Autumn brings an abundant display of red hips that last well into winter.

# Shady gardens

People often talk about shade as if it were the worst of all gardening difficulties. It's true that what will grow in a garden overhung by large trees or shaded by tall buildings may be limited, but there are things you can do to help lighten the darkness. Choosing the right plants makes all the difference – remember that some very beautiful plants are shade-lovers.

## Shade under trees

Dense shade under trees can be a problem, because as well as making the garden dark, the trees mop up moisture and goodness from the soil, leaving nothing to sustain your precious plants underneath. It may be worth consulting a qualified tree surgeon about raising or thinning the crowns of the trees to let in more light. Don't despair, though, when it comes to planting. Many spring bulbs and natural woodland plants (*see* pages 118–19) are perfectly adapted to life under trees, and if you keep them well supplied with what they need by watering and mulching, you won't go wrong.

## Shade from buildings

Many town gardens consist of a small plot shaded by large buildings, which may seem like an insoluble problem. But in gardening terms this kind of shade is easier to work with than shade under trees.

Dealing with shade in these circumstances begins when you're planning the hard landscaping. Think in terms of pale colours to reflect the maximum amount of light. This also applies to your house: white doors and window frames will act as bright focal points when seen from the garden. Cream or white rendered walls – on the boundary or the house – will also reflect light. When considering paving, avoid drab grey-green colours and opt for warm, golden hues instead.

Suggesting a pergola or arbour in a shady garden may seem to be making the problem worse, but you could paint that cream, too. You should be prepared for more frequent repainting than with bare wood or a dark colour, but that is a small price to pay. If you plant it up with deciduous climbers, they will let the sunlight in for six months of the year but give you a beautiful, leafy retreat for hot summer days.

### Shade-loving stalwarts

*Bergenia* cultivars
*Cyclamen hederifolium*
*Epimedium* cultivars
*Euonymus fortunei* 'Emerald 'n' Gold'
*Galium odoratum* (sweet woodruff)
*Geranium macrorrhizum* 'Album'
*Helleborus foetidus*
*Hosta* cultivars
*Iris foetidissima*
*Luzula sylvatica* 'Marginata'
*Sarcococca confusa*
*Tolmiea menziesii* 'Taff's Gold'

Unwelcome in the wild, Spanish bluebells (*Hyacinthoides hispanica*) are irrepressible in gardens.

*See* page 128 for Key to symbols.

# Plants that thrive in a shady garden

## *Euphorbia amygdaloides* var. *robbiae*

● ❖ SPRING

H 50cm (20in) S indefinite

This is one of that valuable group of plants for places where you think nothing will grow. Once established, it gives dense, dark-green ground cover all year, erupting, in early spring, into a froth of flowerheads of the freshest acid lime-green. It goes particularly well with dark-blue or purple flowers such as periwinkles and violets.

## *Fatsia japonica*

● ⬇⬇ ❖ YEAR-ROUND

H 2m (6ft) S 2m (6ft)

There's nothing quite like this plant – except its more ivy-like hybrid offspring, x *Fatshedera lizei*. Both are wonderful architectural plants for shade. *Fatsia japonica*, with its huge, shiny leaves, makes a great focal point (and is fine in a large pot) while x *Fatshedera* is more of a climber. Both look good growing from a carpet of contrasting foliage such as ferns and variegated hostas.

## *Pulmonaria* 'Lewis Palmer'

◑ ⬇⬇ ❖ SPRING

H 30cm (12in) S 30cm (12in)

There are many different pulmonaria cultivars, but this has to be one of the best. Its large, rich blue flowers appear in early spring, and the white-spotted leaves help brighten shady places after flowering is over. If the foliage gets mildew, just cut all the leaves off and a crop of fresh ones will soon appear.

## *Rubus thibetanus*

● ⬇⬇ ❖ WINTER TO SPRING

H 2m (6ft) S 1.5m (5ft)

Its former cultivar name, 'Silver Fern', aptly describes this upright deciduous shrub (a kind of bramble, but don't dismiss it because of that), with a fountain-like arrangement of upright stems. Each season's its new stems are covered with a white bloom, making them stand out against a dark background, especially in winter. It is very low-maintenance: just remember to cut down its old stems in late spring to make way for new, whiter ones. Don't plant it near a path or seat – it's prickly.

## *Ruscus aculeatus*

Butcher's broom

● ⬇⬇ ❖ WINTER TO SPRING

H50cm (20in) S 90cm (3ft)

You will sometimes find this British native growing wild in shady woods, but it is seen more and more in gardens. It is a rather spiky-leaved evergreen shrub with tiny star-shaped flowers. The female form has splendid, large red berries in winter. Some nurseries also sell a hermaphrodite form, which doesn't need a male partner to bear fruit.

## *Vinca difformis*

Periwinkle

● ❖ WINTER TO SPRING

H 30cm (12in) S indefinite

Never waste lovely rich soil on the larger periwinkles like *Vinca difformis* and *Vinca major* cultivars – they will repay you by growing with such vigour that they will soon begin to overwhelm their neighbours. But like the versatile euphorbia (*see* top left) they will put up with poor conditions and make a weed-smothering carpet. *Vinca difformis* has very pale bluish-white, starry flowers that will light up a dark corner. *Vinca major* flowers are violet-blue.

# Windy gardens

It's easy to underestimate the destructive power of wind in a garden. Even light winds can damage young plants and slow their growth, and gardeners on exposed sites know only too well the frustration of constant battles against prevailing winds.

Many of us will occasionally suffer gale damage to trees or buildings, especially now that climate change is bringing more frequent bouts of rough weather. All in all, creating shelter is becoming more important than ever, and giving this a bit of thought at the planning stage can turn your garden into a far more pleasant space – for both you and your plants.

## Wind direction

In the UK, the strongest winds tend to come from the west and south-west. If you are making a new garden on an exposed site, you will probably need to create shelter on that side of the garden first, to give your new plants protection from harsh gales.

Cold air is also worth taking into account, and planting for shelter on the north and east sides of your garden will help to reduce the effects of cold winds and frosty air. Some springtime favourites – for instance, magnolias, camellias and lilac – are particularly susceptible to frosts. Fruit trees, too, will crop less heavily – or not at all – if the blossom suffers frost damage. Giving plants like these a sheltered site may save their flowers from being browned and disfigured by frosty nights at the wrong time.

It is often assumed that town gardens will be sheltered, but tall buildings and the gaps between them can sometimes give rise to unexpected eddies and turbulence that can be quite detrimental. Whatever your situation, take time to notice the prevailing winds in your garden and the problems they cause, so that you can remedy the situation effectively.

## Creating shelter

Fencing may not be the best choice for a very exposed boundary. A solid fence, especially, will be vulnerable to gale damage unless very strongly built. More important, a solid barrier can create a surprising amount of turbulence on its 'sheltered' lee side.

Broom, red and white valerian, seakale and California poppies contribute to a colourful and tough planting scheme for a seaside garden.

In windy places, semi-permeable fencing is better. This might be posts and rails, 'hit-and-miss' fencing, woven hurdles, sturdily fixed trellis, or a picket fence – though not all of these provide much privacy.

A hedge, or – depending on the space available – a mixed shelter belt of trees and shrubs, offers the best of both worlds. It forms an opaque barrier (once it is mature) and it provides very good shelter because it effectively filters the wind, slowing it down and reducing its force without creating eddies on the lee side. A windbreak such as a mixed hedge will effectively protect the plants on that side for a surprisingly long distance – up to ten times the height of the windbreak.

## Seaside gardens

Coastal gardens are a special case and lend themselves to particular plants. Strong, salty winds and, usually, little tree cover for shelter or shade, mean that plants have to take everything that the sea can throw at them, and this rules out many traditional garden favourites. But the advantages of seaside gardens include brilliant light, more equable temperatures, less occurrence of fungal disease and fewer problems with difficult shade. The coasts of south-west England have some enviable gardens that are home to all sorts of exotics and other plants that would struggle inland, and the tempering effect of the sea is felt even in gardens facing into cold easterly winds. Hebes, lavateras, escallonias, fuchsias and hydrangeas are among the shrubs that usually enjoy seaside life. Trees can be difficult to establish, but hawthorns and pines are reliable or, for something more unusual, try eucalyptus or the feathery tamarisk.

*See* page 128 for Key to symbols.

# Wind-tolerant plants

## *Cotoneaster horizontalis*
⇊ ❖SUMMER TO WINTER
H 1.2m (4ft) S 2m (6ft)

Cotoneasters are sometimes dismissed as boring but they are stalwarts in difficult conditions. Bees love them, and there are abundant berries to cheer you and the birds in winter. The small-leaved *Cotoneaster horizontalis* can be grown as a freestanding low shrub or against a wall, perhaps with a wind-tolerant climber such as *Clematis tangutica* trained through it for summer interest.

## *Euphorbia polychroma*
○ ⇊ ❖SPRING TO AUTUMN
H 30cm (12in) S 50cm (20in)

This widely available euphorbia puts up with all manner of adverse conditions. Its acid-yellow flowerheads stay looking presentable from spring through to autumn, by which time the leaves have taken on coral tints. It appreciates some sunshine and good drainage, and is compact enough not to get blown over by the wind.

## *Geranium* 'Ann Folkard'
○ ⇊ ❖SUMMER TO AUTUMN
H 50cm (20in) S 1.2m (4ft)

A long flowering season and striking black-eyed magenta flowers make this vigorous perennial a reliable and attractive choice for mixed borders. It has a scrambling habit, weaving among other plants for support, and is particularly useful for covering the dying foliage of spring bulbs. It dies back to a central crown in winter, so it is not permanently invasive.

## *Hippophae rhamnoides*
Sea buckthorn
○ ⇊ ❖SUMMER TO WINTER
H 3m (10ft) S 3m (10ft)

This resilient shrub combines an iron constitution with an elegant exterior. Its narrow silver leaves suggest a delicate treasure but its natural habitat is by the sea and it puts up with gales and poor soil uncomplainingly. Grow several in a group if you have space. You will need males and females growing together so that you (and the birds) will benefit from orange berries in autumn.

## *Juniperus communis*
○ ⇊ ❖YEAR-ROUND
H and S vary according to cultivar

Windy hillsides are fine for most junipers, which come in an array of shapes and sizes, from ground-covering *Juniperus communis* 'Green Carpet' to the tall, slender 'Hibernica' and 'Schneverdingen Goldmachangel' (above), similar in form to 'Hibernica' but more yellow. *Juniperus communis* 'Compressa' stays as a neat flame shape 60cm (2ft) high, working well in pots.

## *Rosa rugosa*
○ ⇊ ❖SUMMER TO AUTUMN
H 1.5m (5ft) S 1.5m (5ft)

Most pests and diseases are unknown to this vigorous, hip-bearing rose and its cultivars (above, 'Alba'). It has single or double blooms, pink, magenta or white, with crinkly foliage. *Rosa spinosissima* (formerly *Rosa pimpinellifolia*), the burnet rose, also tolerates wind.

# Dry gardens

Dry gardens are not all bad news – far from it. Light, sandy and chalky soils warm up faster than heavy clay in spring and are much easier to work, especially in damp weather. However, very free-draining soils are susceptible to summer droughts. As ever, the answer lies in the soil – and in the planting.

## Improve your soil

There is a lot that you can do to improve dry, free-draining soils. Start by digging in all the organic matter you can – your own garden compost, well-rotted animal manure or a proprietary soil conditioner (now available through council-run composting schemes). Adding humus helps the soil hang on to any moisture that comes its way. Mulching is also important. A surface mulch applied in late winter, before the soil dries out, makes all the difference in the critical spring growing season, ensuring that plants coming out of dormancy have moisture when they need it most. You can use a woodchip mulch (again, try your local council), chipped bark, compost or even grit or slate chippings. Replenish it when it gets thin. Anything that reduces evaporation from the soil will help. A surface covering like this will also make your garden look well tended, setting off your plants to perfection as well as keeping down weeds.

Subtle colours and contrasting shapes combine in this thoughtfully composed planting scheme for a gravel garden.

## Choose the right plants

Many of the plants we grow in our gardens hail from climates much warmer and drier than ours, so when choosing plants for dry gardens it's much better to go for things that would, given the choice, actually prefer to live that way. Top of the list are probably plants from Mediterranean climates, a category that includes many herbs and other aromatic shrubs, spiky or grey-leaved perennials, and bulbs. These are well adapted to managing without water: some have succulent leaves that retain water, others have waxy or leathery leaves that resist evaporation, or silvery, hairy ones to protect them from the sun.

Plants are often overlooked as a tool for retaining soil moisture, but ground-covering shrubs and perennials make a very effective living green mulch, covering and shading the soil in just the same way as well-rotted organic matter.

*See* page 128 for Key to symbols.

## Star performers for a dry garden

### Euphorbia myrsinites
○ ◌ ‖ ❖SPRING
H 15cm (6in) S 45cm (18in)

Euphorbias are the stars of the dry garden, with dazzling, lime-green flowerheads that are a welcome feature in early spring. *Euphorbia myrsinites* has succulent leaves that make it especially drought-tolerant – good for the front of a bed on top of a retaining wall. (Wear gloves when you cut euphorbias, as their sap is a skin irritant.)

### Rosa 'Roseraie de l'Haÿ'
○ ◌ ‖ ❖SUMMER
H 2m (6ft) S 1.5m (5ft)

Attempting to grow roses on poor, dry soil can be frustrating, but try this one. It can make a big bush, but if you have the space it's one of the best for adverse conditions, even resisting blackspot and greenfly. Ideal for the back of a bed, it has a long season of fragrant, double magenta flowers and slightly crinkly, fresh green foliage. Trim and dead-head it occasionally during the summer.

### Rosmarinus officinalis
○ ◌ ‖ ❖YEAR-ROUND
H and S vary according to cultivar

This old-fashioned aromatic shrub comes in many different guises. *Rosmarinus officinalis* 'Miss Jessopp's Upright' does what it says on the tin, while 'Severn Sea' is compact, low and arching, with bright blue flowers. All types of rosemary love warm, dry conditions and poor soil.

### Sedum 'Herbstfreude'
○ ◌ ‖ ❖AUTUMN TO WINTER
H 50cm (20in) S 90cm (3ft)

Commonly known by its English name 'Autumn Joy', this is a real workhorse of a plant. Its contribution lasts for months, from succulent grey foliage, then coral-coloured plates of flowers in late summer, to bronze seedheads in the winter. Plant several – that way, your borders won't look as if they have lost the plot in late summer.

### Sisyrinchium striatum
○ ◌ ‖ ❖SUMMER
H 50cm (20in) S 30cm (12in)

This easy, 'spiky' plant has fans of sword-shaped leaves that add structure, and produces stems studded with cream flower bobbles that blend well with just about everything. For something a bit special try the variegated cultivar *Sisyrinchium striatum* 'Aunt May'.

### Tulipa 'Ballerina'
○ ◌ ‖ ❖SPRING
H 50cm (20in) S 15cm (6in)

Tulips like nothing better than a good baking, and in the right conditions this tall, elegant orange variety will thrive year after year.

# Damp gardens

On a hot summer's day, as you trudge round with a watering can, the idea of a damp garden might sound idyllic. But for a lot of people, a damp garden means clay – probably the most detested of all soil types: sticky and stodgy and crippling to dig, flooding easily and suffocating all but the most amphibious of plants. Yes, clay can be a pain, and it can be hard work to make something of it. But clay that has been successfully improved and well worked gives very good results, making a fertile, moisture-retentive soil that will support a wide variety of plants.

Eupatoriums, rudbeckias and persicarias – all moisture-lovers, here joining forces for an autumn display in Beth Chatto's damp garden.

## Improving the soil

Most damp soils contain clay particles; these are very small and create a dense, heavy, airless mass. The answer is to mix in coarse materials to break the soil up and help it to drain better. Adding grit – sold in garden centres as horticultural grit or coarse grit – will open up the soil structure and improve drainage. Digging in organic matter helps too, so add home-made compost or any other soil-improving source of humus. This will also encourage worms – always a good thing, particularly in heavy soil where the tunnels they make will improve aeration and drainage.

## Laying drainage

In extreme cases, it may be necessary to improve the situation using structural methods such as laying land drains and soakaways. This works both for persistent damp spots and for entire damp gardens – though it can involve serious toil. However, it is only worth doing on sloping sites, because if the waterlogged ground is level there won't be anywhere for the water to drain away. You might just have to get used to wearing wellingtons, and to growing plants that enjoy these conditions.

## Moisture-loving plants

That takes care of the back-breaking bit. Now for the good news. There are dozens of plants that love having wet feet, and you'll make life far less frustrating for yourself if you choose these for your damp garden. Just one word of warning, though. Many damp-loving plants do grow very fast, so keep an eye on the thuggish ones and don't let them smother more delicate neighbours.

### Trees for damp gardens

*Alnus incana* 'Aurea'
*Alnus glutinosa* 'Imperialis'
*Amelanchier lamarckii*
*Betula nigra*
*Crataegus laevigata*
*Gleditsia triacanthos* 'Sunburst'
*Mespilus germanica*
*Sorbus aucuparia*

### Slug and snail control

Unfortunately, damp gardens tend to be popular with slugs and snails. These days conventional slug pellets are increasingly frowned on because they may also harm other creatures, but there are less damaging alternatives, from biological control to copper bands. Natural predators of slugs and snails include frogs and toads, slow-worms, ground beetles, thrushes and hedgehogs, so encouraging these allies will help control the problem. You can make choice areas less attractive to slugs and snails by spreading grit, and keep damp, dark corners tidy so they have fewer breeding places. Torchlight forays to pick slugs off your plants at night, especially after rain, are perhaps the most successful measure, and that way – or by using beer or citrus-peel traps – you have the satisfaction of knowing you've caught the culprits. Lastly, there are plants that slugs don't go for, so try bergenias or *Tellima grandiflora* as ground cover instead of hostas, and grow those plants that are slug delicacies in pots, where it's easier to keep the pests out.

*See* page 128 for Key to symbols.

## Key choices for a damp mixed border

### Cornus alba 'Elegantissima'

○ ◑ ♦ ♦ ❖ YEAR-ROUND
H 2m (6ft) S 3m (10ft)

True to its name, this vigorous dogwood (one of many for damp soil) looks good all year. 'Sibirica Variegata' is very similar but more compact – but either shrub can be kept to size by annual spring pruning, usually removing a third of the stems at the base. This also encourages it to produce glowing red stems – its star feature. Silvery spring buds open into white-variegated leaves.

### Dryopteris wallichiana

● ◑ ♦ ♦ ❖ SPRING TO AUTUMN
H 90cm (3ft) S 75cm (30in)

This deciduous fern has an upright form, with dark brown ribs and scales that are particularly striking against the yellowish green of the emerging fronds. Even when these become darker green, this fern makes a wonderful focal point, planted singly or in groups.

### Eupatorium maculatum Atropurpureum Group

○ ◑ ♦ ♦ pH↑ ❖ SUMMER TO AUTUMN
H 2m (6ft) S 1.2m (4ft)

This tall, hardy clump-former is a good backdrop to a mixed border. It comes into its own in late summer, when it bears clouds of dusty pink flowers. After fading gradually to silvery brown, they stay intact well into winter.

### Persicaria amplexicaulis 'Firetail'

○ ◑ ♦ ♦ ❖ SUMMER TO AUTUMN
H 1.2m (4ft) S 1.2m (4ft)

Useful for making substantial clumps in the middle or back of a border, this robust perennial has glowing, long-lived, pinkish-red pokers.

### Rodgersia aesculifolia

◑ ♦ ♦ ❖ SPRING TO SUMMER
H 1.5m (5ft) S 1.2m (4ft)

The various rodgersias are great architectural foliage plants, which you will be lucky enough to grow only if your soil is moisture-retentive or if you have water to plant them beside. The leaves resemble those of horse-chestnut, and plumes of frothy white or pink flowers are a bonus. Some shade is usually better than full sun.

### Viburnum opulus 'Compactum'

○ ◑ ♦ ♦ ❧ ❖ SPRING AND AUTUMN
H 1.5m (5ft) S 1.2m (4ft)

This is a small version of the native shrub guelder rose, with lobed leaves and hydrangea-like lacecap flowers in spring. These are followed by generous bunches of jammy red, translucent berries that the birds don't seem to want to touch until they're really desperate for food.

# Planning for a green garden

Now that more and more of us want to do our bit to help the planet, making our gardens more eco-friendly is becoming second nature. It's not difficult to improve your environmental credentials as a gardener, especially if you put in some thought at the planning stage.

## Saving water

Climate change has turned water conservation into an issue that now has to be factored into garden planning. We get plenty of rain overall, but usually too much at the wrong time. Storing rainwater to use later helps even things out. Water butts are a relatively cheap and obvious solution and easy to source. Position them, unobtrusively, to catch rainwater from gutters. Laying seep hoses is often recommended as a way of ensuring that the water gets to where it is most needed without wastage. Choosing

This rustic arch is made of sycamore prunings – a completely renewable resource, with a non-existent carbon footprint. And it's free!

## The planet – do your bit

■ Peat is a non-renewable resource, so don't use peat or peat-based composts. Various alternatives that perform well are now available.

■ A plant propagated by a local nursery will have a smaller carbon footprint than one raised in a foreign greenhouse and transported to your garden centre.

■ Try to get hold of locally produced charcoal for barbecues, and support a sustainable woodland industry. Much mass-produced charcoal is made from rainforest timber.

■ Avoid using fertilizer as much as you can. If you choose plants to suit your soil, and use home-made compost, bought-in fertilizers should scarcely be needed. If you do decide to buy fertilizer, avoid inorganic chemicals, which are energy intensive to produce and pollute watercourses with their run-off.

■ Use clay pots wherever possible, and try to find somewhere that takes plastic pots for recycling. There may be a local school or allotment association, or a keen gardener who propagates plants for sale, who could reuse them.

the right plants will make all the difference, too (*see* pages 134–5).

## A softer landscape

When you're planning your hard landscaping, remember that it doesn't have to be literally 'hard', and not everything you build in your garden needs to last for ever. True, there will be times when you want to make a proper job of building something solid and lasting, such as a retaining wall to terrace an awkward slope. But with other features – such as a rustic arch or a play area, or the layout of paths in a kitchen garden – you may fancy a change after two or three seasons. For these, you can take a gentler approach. Instead of 'permanent' materials like concrete and pressure-treated timber – which are difficult to get rid of when you want to make changes – use natural wood (perhaps even home-grown), or free chippings from your own shredder.

## Less power – more peace

Using garden machinery thoughtfully is another aspect of environmentally friendly gardening. Try mowing less often, and allowing wild flowers to colonize longer grass. For small areas, consider a nippy little hand mower. Use shears instead of a strimmer or hedge trimmer, and a good old-fashioned broom instead of a noisy leaf blower or vacuum sweeper. The chances are you'll enjoy the exercise, save money, and the neighbours and local wildlife will appreciate the peace.

## One man's rubbish ...

Recycled construction materials can be a great bargain. If you look out for the best examples, they will lend your garden a maturity that only years of weathering will give to their brand-new counterparts (which may well be the product of unsustainable manufacturing processes). Second-hand bricks, timber and paving slabs are sometimes advertised in local papers or on the internet, and your local council may have recycling centres where such things are sold on very cheaply.

The council may also be the place to go for composts, mulches and soil conditioners. Garden waste collection schemes are gathering pace in many areas, involving vast, high-temperature composting operations. Green waste ultimately becomes an excellent peat-free, weed-free, environmentally friendly compost that is sold, bagged, to enrich people's gardens. Some schemes also produce chipped bark, woodchip mulch and potting compost.

Recycling is all – be it ① a gate built of driftwood or ② compost made from garden and kitchen waste.

## Where is it from?

When you buy anything for the garden, think about where it has come from and what its environmental impact might be. We are getting used to thinking this way about peat and tropical hardwoods such as teak, but not yet, perhaps, about bamboo canes that have been shipped from China, or plastic netting made from petrochemicals. You may well be able to come up with locally produced alternatives – home-grown bamboo or your own woody prunings as plant supports. Dogwood, elder, hazel and buddleia all benefit from a hard cut-back in late winter, producing useful material for poles and pea-sticks, and the cut stems recover very quickly. By the time your supports have become brittle, in a season or two, the shrub will have been obliging enough to grow some more for you. (*See also* page 57.)

## The garden ecosystem

Making your garden more wildlife-friendly is one of the mainstays of green gardening (*see* pages 36–7). Growing a wide variety of different plants is a good start. Other measures to boost a garden's wildlife include making a pond and a compost heap, planting shrubs, hedges and trees for nesting cover, and letting an area of grass grow long. Many of the creatures you'll attract will be predators. These will devour aphids, snails and other plant pests, helping to create a balanced community where pests don't get the upper hand – or at least, not for long. This is a far more sustainable solution than using pesticides, which can harm or kill the beneficial predators as well as the pests.

# Index

Page numbers in *italics* refer to plants illustrated and described in the 'Planting Solutions' chapter.

# Acknowledgements

**BBC Books and OutHouse** would like to thank the following for their assistance in preparing this book: Andrew McIndoe for his advice and guidance; Helena Caldon for picture research; Frederika Stradling for proofreading; Marie Lorimer for the index.

## Picture credits

**Key**   t = top, b = bottom, l = left, r = right, c = centre

**All photographs by Jonathan Buckley** except the following:

**Julia Brittain** 18l, 34t, 112bc, 113br, 131br

**The Garden Collection** Andrew Lawson 40, 73t, 131bc

**iStockphoto** 83r

**Thanks are also due to** the following designers and owners whose gardens appear in the book:

Marylyn Abbott, West Green House, Hampshire 106bl. Maureen Allen, St John's Road, Walsall 8, 29. Gill Brown 104t. Declan Buckley 28, 46. Beth Chatto, Beth Chatto Gardens, Essex 2–3, 15, 42, 85b, 89t, 117t, 136. Mhairi Clutson 112tl. Coughton Court, Warwickshire 115tr. Veronica Cross 98l. Katherine Crouch 47, 110bl. Frances Denby 49. Helen Dillon, The Dillon Garden, Dublin 73t. Fergus Garrett 31b. Stephen Firth & Chichester College students, RHS Chelsea Flower Show 2005 32t. James Fraser 45r. Diarmuid Gavin 33, 55, 64. Graham Gough, Marchants Hardy Plants, East Sussex 122t. Alan Gray & Graham Robeson, East Ruston Old Vicarage, Norfolk 30b.

Maurice Green 11. Robin Green & Ralph Cade 31t, 79l. Growing Ambition, RHS Chelsea Flower Show 2008 112cl. Bunny Guinness 52b, 61. Diana Guy, Welcome Thatch, Dorset 79r. Sue Hayward, RHS Chelsea Flower Show 2008 139l. Simon Hopkinson 73b. Wendy & Leslie Howell 17, 132. Kevin Hughes 126. Paul Kelly 9, 44, 57l. Virginia Kennedy, Rosendale Road, London 30t, 66tr, 100tr, 109br, 113rtl, 113rtr. Rani Lall 25, 52t, 53, 100br. Pam Lewis, Sticky Wicket, Dorset 37bl, 86b, 113br; Christopher Lloyd, Great Dixter, East Sussex 16t, 17tl, 41br, 76, 84, 98r, 99, 100bl, 114bl, 121, 124, 125ct. John Massey, Ashwood Nurseries, Staffordshire 21, 88, 105tr, 113ct, 118l, 118r, 130. Bob Parker, Broad Lane, Wolverhampton, Staffordshire 138. Dan Pearson 89c. Mr & Mrs Guy Rasch, Heale House Garden, Wiltshire 112cb. Sarah Raven, Perch Hill, East Sussex 35, 56, 60, 96l, 97b, 114cr. Nick Ryan 54. Pam Schwerdt & Sibylle Kreutzberger 80. David & Mavis Seeney 90b, 102t. Haruko Seki & Makoto Saito, RHS Chelsea Flower Show 2008 41bl. Shalden Park House 113tl. Gill Siddell 51r. Carol & Malcolm Skinner, Eastgrove Cottage Garden Nursery, Worcestershire 34b, 43br, 83, 102b. Penny Smith 12. Deirdre Spencer 114br. Sue & Wol Staines, Glen Chantry, Essex 90t, 113cb. June Streets 38. Mrs Stuart-Smith, Serge Hill, Hertfordshire 107br. Tom Stuart-Smith: 105tl; RHS Chelsea Flower Show 2005 111. Joe Swift & Sam Joyce for The Plant Room 16b, 45l, 50b, 62r, 92, 105b, 128r. Alan Titchmarsh 112tc, 112r. Xa Tollemache, RHS Chelsea 1997 40. Sue Ward, Ladywood, Hampshire 24, 51l, 78, 86t. Derry Watkins, Special Plants, Wiltshire 117b. Wayford Manor, Somerset 10, 89br, 93c. Cleve West 39t. West Dean Gardens, West Sussex 87t, 107t. Kim Wilde & Richard Lucas, RHS Chelsea Flower Show 2005 57r. Gay Wilson 22b, 101t. Stephen Woodhams 114tr. Sandy Worth, Water Meadow Nursery, Hampshire 4–5, 74–5. Helen Yemm: Eldenhurst, East Sussex 13, 22t, 26, 36, 70l, 72, 112bl; Ketley's, East Sussex 5, 14, 50t, 58t, 70br, 81, 87b 104b, 106tr, 113cr, 116, 134; London 27.